CW00450194

PINK O

An autobiographical look at
How deception operates

Also by Jacques More

Will there be Non-Christians in heaven?
Leadership is Male?
So you think you're chosen?
Revival – The Battleplan
Serious Mistranslations of the Bible
Deleting ELECT in the Bible

PINK OR BLUE

An autobiographical look at
How deception operates

Jacques More

JAROM BOOKS

CONTENTS

MY STORY   1

THE CHARACTERISTICS OF DECEPTION   39

WHICH s/SPIRIT ARE YOU LISTENING TO?   45

OVERCOMING DECEPTION   55

MAKING AN IDOL?   61

PRIDE IS A KILLER   67

WOLF IN SHEEP'S CLOTHING?   73

WOMEN AND DECEPTION   89

MAN'S 1ST SIN IDENTIFIED
PASSIVITY AS HIS WEAKNESS   95

IN CONCLUSION   105

To the memory of John Barr

John was an Elim Minister and ran
Freedom Road Ministries in East London

MY STORY

Peter talked about the pink or blue hydrangeas. Apparently, though often seen with large multi-flowered heads of pink, if you would like this flowering plant to be blue, all you need do is put rusty nails in the soil. That's what he said. So, if you have a garden with two hydrangea plants separated by two different soil types, one in a more alkali based soil than neutral, and another, in a more acid based soil, you would have two beautiful bushes: One pink and one blue.

What an amazing world we live in!

As an illustration this proved powerful, though not realised immediately: A person's heart, if seen as "pink", could go on to grow naturally and become "blue", just by the right input. Meaning, if minded one way, but fed over time appropriately, then a person's view would naturally be changed. And that is exactly how this picture idea was used in my mind by the deceiving spirit in 1981. The spirit suggested this was a word of comfort from God to help me believe someone was to be in my life, who appeared only for the moment, elsewhere in their attention.

Though a Religious Education teacher at *The Wildernesse School*, where I had been a student in Sevenoaks, Peter was perhaps best known in his spare time for his keen gardening.

He regularly spoke of a plant or a flower as I gave him a lift. We would go on to pick up the electric organ on our way to our worship gatherings. This was a piece of furniture really. The more regular slim keyboards of today were not as much in vogue, nor with all the gadgets our organ held. The instrument with solid wooden side panels that acted as its own stand, (only just) fitted in between the wheel arches of the Ford Cortina MkII Estate. So it was great to have Peter's help to lift it in and out and the arrangement ensured he had a ready means to get to and from the fellowship meetings.

I was keen on a local girl named Fiona*. She wore a pretty necklace with a pink stone in the shape of a small heart on the end of it. Fiona had bought it one day at the *Sevenoaks Market* on her way home from school. On the day she bought it she said how she would have preferred buying a blue one she had seen. But, it had been too expensive. Shame I thought, as it would have been a match to her blue eyes. This is where the illustration would come in. I was keen on Fiona, but I could not see her interested. I thought she was interested with someone else called Pete, but when I heard a few years later he was going out with Tracey, I then realised Fiona was free. This is when the deceiving spirit began giving me signs and "making me" believe in Fiona and that her heart would change from pink, just like her necklace, to the preferred and intended "blue".

The enemy, as I call all evil spirits, just like Jesus did in the parables (Matthew 13:25; Luke 10:19), they know the things that we know. These they make use of against us or to divert us from the Lord and His ways. In fact, I was to learn that even the very secret decisions of the heart that one makes in childhood, so very long ago, these are also known by them. They have

*By request a name/some names have been changed.

2

access to that information. And, if it serves their purpose, they will readily make use of that information. When I was a pre-teen boy I remember graduating from sweets to comics with my pocket money. I was born in Holland, then raised up South of Paris in France until the age of 11 when we moved to England. I recall great comic mags like *Spirou* in my early days of reading in French. A little later after we'd moved to England I got English magazines like *Look and Learn* and *World of Wonder*. I remember a friend also gave me a load of back copies. This would have been just a little while before I progressed to a great model making era. But these and especially the later mags were great in teaching me about the world we live in whilst I had fun reading them and catching up on stories. I learned a lot of history, geography, science, technology and not least, a great amount of good English spelling which I sub-consciously absorbed in the process.

One of the things I got to learn from these mags, and got concerned about, was pollution in the midst of the amazing natural world we inhabit which they were describing. I came to love nature so much. Maybe it was the beauty, the wonder and the order in rich "eco-systems" that attracted me. Not that I learned that big word till a little later. I remember going through a phase of having posters of nature, animals, plants, but with one significant omission. All the scenery was without a single man made item within them and, of course, but unwittingly perhaps, no humans anywhere either. As if humans were not part of the world! In my desire not to have anything "artificial" showing in the pictures, I was cutting out the very beings for whom the world was created. Subtle stuff, but this was in my pre-Christian days: a totally un-churched and non religious upbringing.

I'd place these pictures on the walls all around my bedroom. This concern for animal life, nature and how pollution affected it, made me think up and read on how to clean up and protect the world about us. How we should co-exist with nature. I remember at 13 writing an English essay in class on what I would do if I was a rich man: The subject of the essay we were given. I modelled my thinking on the *Thunderbirds* idea of having a rescue centre, but this one with a ready arsenal of all the gear to fight any ecological crisis anywhere in the world: with all the latest equipment on how to salvage wrecks and mop up spilled oil and so on. A few years earlier, as I recognised animals regularly becoming extinct, a theoretical scenario came to my mind and a question. What if, one day, I came across a lion in a jungle? And, knowing the lion species was in threat of extinction – in contrast to the human race and it's suggested over population – What would I do? What could I do? I made a choice there and then, based on the simple logic that the human race would benefit with the lion species still present (in contrast to another human of which there were plenty). I came to this decision: in spite of being armed to defend myself, I chose that in such a situation to willingly lay my life down for the lion. I had never shared this with anyone. But there and then I had made a distinct inner decision in the privacy of my room and stored it in my heart. The deceiving spirit would remind me of that decision made more than a decade earlier and try to make use of it! Though this was well hidden and lost in my distant memory of growing up, out of the blue, this was returned to my mind at a time of being prepared to "Die for the Lord", but more on that shortly.

I made that decision as a pre teen boy. Fiona shared her pink or blue necklace story when I was in my mid teens. Peter and I were driving around when I was twenty three at the time he shared his hydrangea trivia. The enemy had access to all this knowledge that I had experienced and now made use of it all.

One springtime day, round about the same time I learned about hydrangeas, and on our way to the destination of the day with our musical load on board, we observed a whole row of gorse bushes in full bloom. It is likely to have been mid May and I think this was on a stretch of the A25 road on our way to the set up for one of our Sunday morning gatherings. In the latter years of the fellowship we also had a smaller Sunday morning gathering at *Ightham Village Hall*. So there Peter and I went with the musical organ.

The bountiful yellow flowers of the gorse overtook the field of view as we drove by. Peter mentioned another of his anecdotes. He said, even though this was the time of year to see gorse flowers at their most abundant, irrespective of the time of year, they were always found with a flower somewhere in a bush. He said it was due to this there was a saying, "Since, there are always flowers in a gorse bush; there is always love about". I've looked this up since and the original saying is "When the gorse is out of bloom, then kissing is out of fashion". They are one of those few plants in the world that will retain a flower all year round.

What an amazing world!

Soon after Peter shared this I was driving my car on my own one day and the odometer (I've always thought: "What a weird name!") i.e. "The mileage indicator" was coming up to a big number. As children, my sisters and I used to love calling out when the big number turned up on the dial, whilst we were travelling somewhere as a family. This was no digital readout, but a number by number mechanism that turned into place as a car was travelling along. Who was going to be the first to spot it? No prizes: Just a lot of fun. No pocket computer games in those days (none in homes yet). There were plenty of other pastimes including singalongs and chanting the zigs and the zags of left hand and right hand bends of a winding road and spotting things… So it was, with this childhood practise of watching out for the big numbers on the odometer, I did not think it strange that my attention should be drawn to look this day, though I had perhaps not done so for many years. As I inclined to look at the mileage number I noticed that, as this big number turned into existence, right then, exactly at right angles to the car, as I was moving along, there was this gorse bush full of yellow flowers and, equally at the same time, a feeling of recognition of a physical kind swept over me. Like a wave of emotion. I was immediately reminded of what Peter had said, "You know there is always love about because there is always flowers in a gorse bush". The deceiving spirit was doing its work. Not that I knew this is what that was at the time. It would turn out to be months before I learned the true source of these impressions. And, right then, Fiona came to mind. This whole set of events led me to wonder, to pray, and to believe for an "us".

Like other guys my age I had this common crush on long jet black haired Fiona Thompson with the blue eyes and the pink heart on a necklace. Her family had welcomed me as I lived up to six miles away and her home was en route to my bus stop from where I went to school. We both went to a group known as the *Breakdown Gang* which served to support the ministry of Ken Lock who led the fellowship which I began to attend at the age of 15. I did not know then that I would remain part of the fellowship for a further 9 years which is when, in Spring 1982, and quite dramatically, the fellowship ceased. These "Gang" meetings were about once a fortnight on a week night and were separate to the weekly home gatherings where prayer or bible study happened. They were also separate to the main weekend public meetings. The home gatherings were not like the small gatherings in a home more prevalent today with a limited number and then several held at the same time in different homes. In these instead, everyone who could come, did so. All would be made to fit in the one home of the night for the event. Anything from thirty to eighty people all in one home sitting in every nook and cranny possible. Great times of close fellowship. This crammed home gathering is not unlike the gatherings of the underground church behind the iron curtain before the Berlin wall fell. It is just like some of the underground churches in China now, though we here need not do it in secret.

The Breakdown Gang however was a more intimate teaching and sharing time with a select group of younger committed people to the work of Ken and never more than twenty or so. This work of Ken was also known as "The ministry". We were the ministry "inner group". At least that's how we were made to feel, though this was not a governing role, but a supportive and closer teaching set up occasion. These were times of sharing and with access to matters to pray and intercede about.

In my early days Alison Ball who was in her twenties and lived near me in *Brasted* used to give me a lift home in her trusty blue Mini Clubman Estate as she was part of the group too. And before I could drive after passing my test at 18, I would often get a lift home from her or someone else in the group.

At weekends when her brother David came to the full public meetings he would pick me up and drop me off. Sometimes I took the bus to meetings, but always tended to get a lift home, but *Breakdown Gangs* were an early evening get together and held in a home not far from the Thompsons. Seton Clement a biology teacher at *The Wildernesse School* where I went in *Sevenoaks* ran the Christian Union (CU) lunch time get-togethers. Seton first mentioned the fellowship to us boys at the school CU in terms of the Saturday night fortnightly *Young People's* public *meetings* held in any one of the bigger homes of folk in the fellowship. Once a fortnight, the main official public gathering of the fellowship was in *Dunton Green Village Hall*, down the road from Riverhead, all close to Sevenoaks. The nearby M25 and M26 motorways had not yet been built. The latter M26 literally now a stone's throw from the hall. The weekend in between these fortnights there was the Young People's meeting. Though in reality, even though so named, all the folk who came to Dunton Green meetings came to these too. The only difference was the name and it did serve to help Seton when it came to invite youngsters to check it out. Never in a recruitment fashion, but an occasional offer to come along. The whole fellowship was run and led by the ministry of "Ken and Mike". Ken being the lead and main public person, later to be the only lead. Mike helped Ken, and not least, in that Ken was blind and needed a guide to where he needed to sit and walk, etcetera. I have no memory of Mike ever speaking publicly. And in fact a few years into the fellowship Mike was isolated and made to leave. From then on Ken was generally led to the car or mini bus or a chair by any one of the ladies that remained at his side to assist.

In the early days of *The Ministry* Ken and Mike would travel together and offer counsel, prayer and deliverance/ healing sessions for individuals in any one of the several designated ministry homes which belonged to any of the committed faithful adult couples in the fellowship. In later years when a larger home was purchased, this then became the preferred venue for any such private "ministry" meetings during the week days. Some private sessions were highly beneficial to those receiving counsel and ministry. An example of this is when Ken shared one day at a *Breakdown Gang* that the Holy Spirit was amazing in the words of knowledge sometimes imparted. This lady had come for ministry and in Ken's mind the words "3 blind mice" was given him by the Holy Spirit. As the lady was questioned and this was shared she opened up to a whole secret part of her early years she had never shared with anyone else before. This led to this lady being set free from things holding her (back) and to be healed. Then there were later private ministry meetings that were not used for that: times of a fall – Ken had discreet affairs – that were kept hidden and were secret till the final weeks of the fellowship. But none of us got to know about those until Spring 1982. I had by then nearly been a decade in the fellowship.

Ken was a keen Cricket player and being blind ended up doing all the bowling which he was excellent at. His blindness was due to Retinitis pigmentosa which his brother had before him. Ken developed it soon after his children were born. When playing cricket you needed to initially say you were in the crease and that enabled him to have a fix on you. I'll never forget the googly he once threw me in the final years of the fellowship at a boarding school's playing ground at Seaford in Sussex. The place was hired for a week for a summer camp. I remember going at least twice. I probably have played more cricket there than anywhere. I loved it. Ken also played the accordion and all the public gatherings saw him play and lead worship accompanied by the guitars, the organ, and all of us singing. We loved it all and sang with gusto. It was great being part of a group of Christian believers that was growing, where healings were taking place and good teaching was evident. What attracted me in the first place was the full gospel taught and practised. I knew of no other local gathering of Christians that did that. When you become a Christian from an un-churched background and read about the miracles in the time of Jesus and the early church, it motivates you to want to be where it's at: To be somewhere with the "gifts" of the Holy Spirit operating and not denied.

About once a month on a Saturday we did an en mass reach out event in the vicinity of Reading in Berkshire as we were connected with a small fellowship of believers that met at a small village named *Three Mile Cross*. The town of Reading is West of London and is in Berkshire, an official part of the "South East". In the sequence of things this would occur on a *Young People's* Saturday as we called them. A whole group of us would go in threes or fours and knock on people's doors inviting them to the meeting that evening, but best of all we went to talk and listen as we shared about Jesus. I loved talking about the Lord. We never did it in twos as that made us look similar to JWs. I remember one elderly gentleman whose door we knocked on telling us how during WW2 he was involved in a submarine accident (or another military conflict – I can't recall), but as the sub was sinking he said he'd cried out to God and, he does not know how, but somehow he and one other guy were the only survivors (something like that).

When I turned 18 Ken telephoned me at home one day and mentioned about moving into one of the fellowship homes …

It happened like this. At the prayer meetings we had, I would pray for my mum and asking the Lord's help with things at home. More in terms of salvation than anything, if I recall, but as soon as I turned 18 and there was this spare room in one of the fellowship homes, I was invited to live with Keith and Sheila. They lived in a three bed house in Sevenoaks which now belonged to *The Ministry*. The previous bigger family having moved to the larger home then purchased on the other side of town. This invitation was not an option on my part, but in view of my commitment to the ministry, my refusal would be a denial of believing Ken was hearing from the Lord in this matter. This was made clear as I replied to Ken with words like "I'd like to pray/consider this offer" to which I was told by Ken he had already prayed about it. It was a "slam dunk!" as they say.

I had passed my driving test by then, which made going back and forth to meetings easier, and I had embarked in studies at a local College of Further Education. The college was named *West Kent College* and was situated at Tonbridge. I was studying the Diploma in Automobile Engineering which included Motor Retail Trade management and a full knowledge of vehicle functions and combined with practical experience by block release work with local garages. All this ensured a rounded appreciation of cars and the trade. Together with Keith, whose home I now shared, we became a team that carried out free repairs and maintenance in our evenings and weekends for all the ministry vehicles. This meant I had no social time at all. If I wasn't in a meeting, I was working on a car. And, when I finished College and was working full time as a car mechanic, the meetings became my only break from cars. This meant in 1981 that only by a miracle of some kind could anything happen: for any possibility of anyone like Fiona and I to get to hang out, and have a relationship. Prayer was my sole avenue of regular input into this. That was the time of these signs from the deceiving spirit.

Mind you, there was one exception, not in terms of hanging out; just of a time to make a tentative connection, but I think this was well before the full time car period. It was this:

When back at home near *Westerham* and during my last TV watching for a number of years, there had been this commercial ad for Milk Tray chocolates. A guy in the role of a James Bond 007 like character, following the overcoming of numerous obstacles with a helicopter and other paraphernalia, secreted a box of Milk Tray chocolates into this lady's bedroom with the added touch of a card with an emblem of him as the secret admirer and the ad finished with the spoken caption "All because the lady loves Milk Tray". I decided to do the same with Fiona. I bought a box of the chocolates and a card then I planned a means to do it. Not too hard with this home from home, in the moments before a *Breakdown Gang* meeting. The funny thing, I recall Fiona talking of Prince Charles on occasion and what a great guy he was. This was before Charles ever met Lady Di – and, when I placed the box in her room (the only time I ever entered), there was a part of one wall dedicated to pictures of Prince Charles. I never told Fiona and the card was as cryptic as could be: no words if I recall, just an illustration I made: a heart pierced through with an arrow...

Back to the later story. The prayers I made then involved my praying for Fiona's heart to turn from pink to blue as the Lord fed her since I was not confident that she was interested, but nevertheless believed this was "the Lord" indicating this to me. Not that there were as mentioned, any private or social times to enable a chat and discover at all about any interest, but this is how it played out in my mind. Since there were no social contact and interaction opportunities, I indeed felt prayer was my only avenue of progress.

As I prayed daily and more for Fiona, a pattern of regular "coincidences" occurred. The odometer readings and the yellow flowers which would immediately be visible at exactly right angles to the car would manifest. It didn't matter what car I drove. It happened without fail time and time again. And, as a car mechanic I drove many cars. I remember one Saturday which was the monthly trip to Reading I was on the rota to work till noon at Caffyns in Sevenoaks where I then worked. After I finished college I worked for this firm – one of the oldest garage firms historically having begun soon after the invention of the horseless carriage – but in their newly acquired site next to the newly built Police Station on the Sevenoaks road to Riverhead (there's a big Lidl's supermarket there now). Riverhead is a local crossroad of routes: where the A21 and the A25 once crossed. I could not get out of this Saturday rota. All the swapping possibilities had been exhausted. And, what had been a monthly outreach trip, for Keith and myself who were (now) the car boys, this was now a day to work on the cars for the Reading folk. I missed not going door to door (I loved it!). Graham who had joined our "team" (we never called it that) had become the (car) bodyshop guy whilst Keith and I were the mechanics. There were other "teams" too like the gardening team and the decorating team, but these were less constant than the car team which was permanent and the only one active on a Reading Saturday. The practical needs of all were well met in the fellowship. No one had an unmet need. It was organised that day, as soon as I could get away from work, I would drive Graham's car a lighter blue Cortina MkIII Estate already loaded up with gear straight to Reading. I noted his mileage counter coming up to a big round number so by the time I got on the M4 motorway, sure enough, it turned to that complete amount. I was doing bang on the speed limit of 70MPH as I was conscious that was the right thing to do and, you know what? In spite of mile upon mile of greenery, right there, at right angles to the car, it was bang on! At the turn of the mileage was this whole field full of yellow flowers: amazing!

I got to the designated home whose forecourt allowed sufficient room for a car to be jacked up and already one was put on stands for us to service. It was a Morris Marina that day: One of the several which fellowship folk owned. Then, as the afternoon progressed it became apparent some more parts were going to be needed. We knew every place wherever we were that had available goods for car maintenance and how late they were open. When back in Kent, perhaps the farthest we travelled for a part, so a car would still get fixed the same day, was Stockwell Motors in Clapham Road. They were open till 10 at night if I remember. Keith tended to handle the parts money and Graham needed to go and pick out some bodywork materials. So this day at Three Mile Cross I got on with the car service on my own. There I was alone under this car in my overalls and two things then happened. I heard an assembly of birds singing and gusts of wind. Intrigued I looked out from underneath the car in the direction of a home on the other side of the road. What I then saw stuck with me. It was unusual to hear gusts of wind and have a whole apex of a roof lined up by a row full of birds. Then I noticed the name of this property was *Windsmeet*. And, to top it all the small front garden had both pink and blue hydrangea bushes and the rest of the flowers were all yellow!

What was going on?!

And why was I the only one experiencing these things? (Mind you, how could I know that? I never shared this with anyone! Yet) In the middle of it all – all that you experience and the things that you feel – you don't think objectively. You may feel you are, but instead of really permitting any real critique and, with these experiences you get a sense, a feeling this is really personal, private, and it is unsafe to share it with anyone. As if sharing it would remove the possibility of losing what you have been given or was about to have (as "promised" or indicated).

At this point I had experienced many dramatic coincidences. As well as a multitude of direct answers to questions asked in prayer. Not a few bible passages were given me as back up to these coincidental experiences. Verses suddenly relevant were "given" by an opening to the right page and eyes immediately falling on the right portion (out of context, of course). And time and again with the radio played at work you "identified" emotionally with songs that were connected to this reality presented by the spirit like "It won't be long, yea, till I belong to you…" But, what a Saturday this was turning out to be!

We finished off the work we could do on the cars and got ready for the evening meeting at the Three Mile Cross venue. That evening a sense of a shift was brought to my attention from the spirit's regular encouragement to keep committed and (just believing) that Fiona and I would be an item. The passage of the bible for that evening, as well as various songs, they were all about our gathering together with the Lord in the air. In 1 Thessalonians 4 Paul wrote about the time when the dead in Christ – those who knew the Lord on earth, but died before Jesus' return – would be resurrected and gather with Jesus in the air and there would be met by all the other saints, all believers still alive on earth, but "raptured" (gathered together also) to this meeting at the day of His return. It is a passage of Scripture that explains there will be a "meeting in the air" prior to then coming down with Jesus to His return to earth to rule with Him from Jerusalem. Paul said:

> **For this we say to you by the word of the Lord, that we who are alive *and* remain until the coming of the Lord will by no means precede those who are asleep. For the Lord Himself will descend from heaven with a shout, with the voice of an archangel, and with the trumpet of God. And the dead in Christ will rise first. Then we who are alive *and* remain shall be caught up together with them in the clouds to meet the Lord in the air. And thus we shall always be with the Lord.**
>
> *1 Thessalonians 4:15-17*

Wow! I thought. That agrees with the name of that house with all the birds singing on top of it. This meeting place in the air could be aptly named as where the "Windsmeet"! After all there was this separate passage also talking of the rapture in terms of God sending angels to gather the saints from the four winds (Matthew 24:31).

We probably also sang one of our favourite hymns, though I can't remember, but this fits the pattern I am describing:

"There's going to be a meeting in the air . . . In the sweet, sweet, bye and bye…"

This was a lot to take in. Was the Lord now telling me someone was going to die? Was I?

Were Fiona and I then to be together at this place (yes?) but not on earth, but later, "Where the winds meet?" Is this what I was being told?

This was a serious change of direction. I felt I needed something more concrete from the Lord. So I asked him.

Now, in all the meetings that were held, time was always given for anyone with a word of prophecy or a tongue and then an interpretation. A freedom was there to practise what Paul had taught the Corinthians: Give room for 2 or 3 of these in your meetings and then a discernment is to be made of what has just been heard:

> **But now, brethren, if I come to you speaking with tongues, what shall I profit you unless I speak to you either by revelation, by knowledge, by prophesying, or by teaching?**
>
> **If anyone speaks in a tongue, *let there be* two or at the most three, *each* in turn, and let one interpret. But if there is no interpreter, let him keep silent in church, and let him speak to himself and to God. Let two or three prophets speak, and let the others judge.**
>
> *1 Corinthians 14:6, 27-29*

Up to that point I had not shared what I was getting with anyone. There is one exception I'll explain soon. This Fiona thing was personal after all. But I had been trusting what the Lord said regularly through the "gifts" in the meetings. And, *except* for this next word, none had been in line with the deceiving spirit; though none prevented it as yet. The next big public get together was going to be at our fortnightly *Dunton Green Village Hall* get together. So I asked the Lord, if this was Him, and if He was telling me He was taking me home early (I was 23 remember), then I was asking Him to mention the word "death" through a gift of the Spirit at that next meeting. Words of prophecy or, a gift of tongues and an interpretation, all fall under the name of *gifts of the Spirit* (1 Corinthians 12:1) and, as indicated these were regularly practised in our meetings – this is the common name for the abilities by the Holy Spirit which Paul writes about in 1 Corinthians 12, but accurately he named only one with that name, "**gifts of healings**" (1 Corinthians 12:9). Only the Lord and I were aware of this challenge, this question I posed. It was not my first time of communicating this way with the Lord, but perhaps this was the first explicit request by the means of a particular word being mentioned. So, this next Saturday I got there as normal with Peter and the organ. We had an extended time of worship that night and to my surprise not only was the word "death" mentioned but also "marriage" as in the marriage of the Lamb. Wow! I thought. This really was God speaking to me…

The Lord had spoken. I was going to die – The Lord was going to take me home! (the phrase used by Christians) – I started to do a lot of tidying up. It is amazing the amount of stuff we keep which we never really have any use for. Even more so, if you know you only have weeks to live. But, actually, how long I had, I did not get to recognise until I asked about that too, though perhaps not as consciously this time. The hurdle, this shift – of emphasis – had now been crossed, but the spirits at work carried on. I was road testing a car out of *Caffyns*. I often drove a circular route that took me on the A25 approach back to Riverhead on my return back to the shop. I have a picture in my memory of road testing an SD1 Rover as I was often given work on them and on that stretch of road seeing a car in front with a number plate with "Job 105". And, since nothing happens by chance and (then) I took that to mean "Everything must happen by God." – though in truth, yes, nothing happens by chance, but this does not equal to "everything happens by God." There are many free willed choices not in line with God's will – but I was not conscious of that in the midst of my need and the deception (and, no one wants to hear what they do not want to hear!) – I took special note of "Job 105" and resolved to look this up. I had seen no change to my daily life and status quo for some time and, a longing for more, made me fertile ground for an idea that glory itself (heaven) was soon to be my future. The change of hope from more life here to, more life there, had caught me. Fiona was no longer in the forefront; it was the end goal now. To make the point this was a "happening of God" I was now being given a when. This is how Job 10:5 reads in the KJV "***Are* thy days as the days of man? *are* thy years as man's days**". At 23 "my days" as "my years" was a simple proposition. The 23rd was the date! We were now at the beginning of September 1981. This was going to be the glorious day! The day of meeting my Lord and being with Him forever! The end of my toil! The end of a life limiting existence of only eating, sleeping and working on cars (though this was only a feeling in part since I loved serving). But there was precious little balance. So with my trusty blue *Cortina MkII Estate* I made not a few trips to the tip and began to get rid of all I owned or had kept that was superfluous. I managed this in that the local tip opened early and I could make a trip there in good time before I got to work each day.

I wrote my dad a letter. Within I stated this might be my last letter to him. I was the only one in touch with him anyway. My parents split and divorced when we were little and after my mum, sisters and I moved to England, and having become a Christian at 14, I took my responsibility seriously to "honour my parents" (from Ephesians 6:2). In this disconnected family situation this meant I was the only one who had re-made and then kept contact with my dad. I now wrote in this letter how he needed Jesus since I wanted to be faithful in having told him about the Lord for the last time, but I also said this may be my last letter(!). Years later he told me that when he received that letter he wished he'd had the capacity to drop everything and come over.

I was also encouraged to share of this great event to others by the passage from Ezekiel given me by the spirit "**And they, whether they will hear, or whether they will forbear, (for they *are* a rebellious house,) yet shall know that there hath been a prophet among them.**" (Ezekiel 2:5 KJV). "**they will know that a prophet has been among them**" was repeated in my head. It was another one of those verses that just "happened" for my eyes to have fallen on as I just "happened" to open up my bible to that section of text. Like the other "affirming texts" I'd been getting. This passage meant that, though the people may not realise it now, as I was sharing with them of "this great upcoming event", they would realise when it happened, that there had been a prophet in their midst. So I began to share of this great news coming up on the 23rd with everyone at work…

Could this also have proved my salvation(?)…

One bolder apprentice started asking questions about this event. I had not told anyone I was actually going to die. But his curious (mischievous?) probing however made me say things that enabled him to put two and two together and he went and had a chat with the Branch manager. The Branch Manager, responsibly and reasonably, called me into his office for a chat. I remember explaining how I lived by the old Roman "law of the slate" (something I had heard someone say): you live a normal life never knowing, if or when, a slate might fall off a roof as you pass by, thus enabling you to live your life to the full and constantly in the moment. Phew! That was a close one.

But the Lord really did have people in place to prevent anything happening, and these *were* my salvation. The fellowship home in Sevenoaks with the biggest driveway and a two car space garage was the best place where most of the evening and weekend car work got done. The property had been called *Shalom* and the East family and several older ladies also resided. Gordon was a retired school headmaster and in the preceding weekend to my big day, which according to the calendar was due to happen on the Wednesday of that upcoming week, during a tea break of that car weekend, Gordon shared in private with me a secret of his. I felt obliged to reciprocate and share a secret of mine. So I mentioned my secret crush with Fiona, but explained how I felt the Lord was moving me on, to better things (or something similar). I did not specify. Then there was Abi and Andrew who came by with regard to work on their car – it was either their earlier Hillman Imp or their later R4, I can't remember, and their car was booked to be done that Wednesday evening – but Andrew said something like "See you on Wednesday" and I (of course) could not say that I would… I had by then also got another impression about this "great event". This was going to happen in the lunchtime of the Wednesday: the 23rd! All car work for the ministry cars in the week was in the evenings. So, I could not say I'd be there…

After those preceding weekend conversations, the next fellowship meeting due was the Tuesday bible study night. This either happened in a home in Tonbridge or the Thomson's: Fiona's home. And this very Tuesday it was her place too!

Now, earlier in the year, in the Spring, Ken had fasted for several weeks. At the end of this time he had become weak and he unexpectedly died. Ken had been the head and total leader of the fellowship. But as regards finances and purchases, like the homes and some of the cars, things had been handled through a charity named the *Earmark Trust* with Charles Raven as a trustee. Charles with his wife Liz had a home near Ightham where various meetings were sometimes held. Charles then became the active head of the fellowship.

Ken shared in his final weeks more personal stuff. He mentioned how he'd had a heart to heart with the Lord. And how he had confessed things to the Lord and that the blood of the Lamb – Jesus is described by John the Baptist in the bible as the Lamb of God who takes away the sin of the world (John 1:29) – Ken said the blood had covered his sins. This he said at the last bible study night with him at the Thomson's. Ken did not specify what he'd confessed. All this was during this fasting time. To his daughter Val in his final days there were moments he kept saying "I'm sorry". As a regular practise for years in my daily devotions I had come to bind the enemy in Jesus' name in and around Ken. And in one of my last memories of him at Shalom where I worked on the cars we had an unusual chat. The house toilet we used downstairs was an internal room that required a light on every time you used it. So with light showing under the door I always knew if someone else was in the room if I needed to go. I needed to go and saw no light, so I tried the door. It was locked (!?). I looked again and sure enough, there was no light. So, unsure if I had (really) tried to open the door properly, I tried again. Sure enough it was locked. Then, I heard the door being unlocked and Ken came out. Of course, being blind he'd had no need for light. He asked who had been trying the door. I explained how I had seen no light so I tried the door. And seeing the light was really not on, I'd tried the door again. His response in the moment was quite emotional and this may have been the most humble expression I ever witnessed from him. He thanked me for things and moved on to the room nearby. Perhaps it was as if this issue of light not being seen, spoke to him as an allegory? That's how it can seem now in hindsight. A parallel expression of what he had gone through internally. Ken died within days of that.

My last memory of Ken was his sharing a "joke" with me the evening before he died. He died either in the night or the early hours of the next morning. The white Ford Transit 12 seater mini bus, which was used to ferry folk from Streatham where Ken and family lived and on to the many venues, had a broken rear suspension leaf spring. The crack was spotted on the Sunday. Keith and I obtained the part and travelled up to fit it in the front of the house on the Monday or Tuesday evening. We did the job and Keith was not present as I perhaps was in the house passing through after washing my hands. Ken and I had a brief exchange of words by the door of the front room. I mentioned how we'd done the job. Ken asked how much it had been (remember the money was Keith's department, but I knew the price of the part). I mentioned how much it was. He then joked how the shares would fall tomorrow! He died that night.

The news of Ken's death was a shock to us all. That morning – ahead of hearing the news – I woke with the clear still small voice of the Holy Spirit with the words of the verse "**Greater love hath no man than this, that a man lay down his life for his friends.**" (John 15:13 KJV). Some time later, I shared this with John of *Three Mile Cross* and he mentioned how that morning he too woke up with a verse given him: "**The good shepherd gives His life for the sheep.**" (John 10:11). The long and short of it, as I see it all in retrospect, I believe Ken did everything he could with the Lord to put things right before his departure. And my understanding is he knew he was going. The time then given to the fellowship from his death till the final gathering of the fellowship – nearly a year – was time to prepare many for the news to come. His final weeks fasting and intercession enabled that. He stood in the gap on our behalf before going (Ezekiel 22:30).

In the months that followed Ken's death, Charles and I had a private chat. He was doing this with everyone. I mentioned my interest in Fiona. He said how he had come to a point where he was not in a position to judge or make decisions over things without spending some time asking the Lord. Or, words to that effect (Respect!). And, later in the summer, he came over to *Shalom* one weekend and said to me words like "I see no green lights over this". To which I replied – since I had pictured Fiona's heart as pink and being turned blue over time, with the Lord's feeding like the hydrangea plant, I said – "I agree. I think it is amber and needs time …" Charles did not press the issue (Respect again!). And, at the time, I was getting plenty of yellow flower reminders with any mileage of value! I had not shared that (!), yet …

So, on Tuesday 22nd September as I walked up to the front door of Fiona's home on my way to the meeting there that evening Charles was there early, waiting for me. He suggested we went into the Study. I was unusually early too. This meeting would be the last time Charles and I would really properly share privately together. There was nothing to forewarn that. I think this went on to be because another occasion would also entail discussing again things that would (perhaps) be too difficult to cope with: the whole issue of being deceived can be troubling. We took up about two thirds or most of the evening time to talk. To talk about something I was to discover hard to face.

Charles started by saying he'd heard some disturbing things from Andrew and Gordon arising from my conversations with them at the weekend and, in his own praying seriously since, the Lord had given him two words "**seducing spirit**" (also named as "**deceiving spirits**" in 1 Timothy 4:1 contrasting KJV with NKJV). It was not something he could say much more about, but it was all that was needed. This is the beauty of a word of knowledge. It enabled me to open the door. I took time to spill the beans in the Thomson's study with just the two of us present. I did share all with him this time. However, my immediate reply to the words "seducing spirit" was "I can believe this – that it was a deceiving spirit (even if, as yet, I did not understand how or why) – but I only could believe it, (yes, only if…), if the Lord had a hand in this." I was referring, of course, to the word "death" mentioned in the "word" as I had asked of the Lord specifically. This part had to have been with the Lord's involvement… I ended our time agreeing that there was nothing from the ordinary that I would carry out doing in the days ahead. On the Wednesday – the very next day – I promised and determined there would be no change from the norm, that I was going to do. If the Lord was taking me home, then it had to be His doing. I had nothing consciously to do to contribute to it. As we finished our unusual meeting and then rejoined everyone else, as usual, the place was packed. I sat in the entrance lobby in the overflow crowd from the living room. It was now the tail end of the evening's gathering. As we sang a few final songs, I could not help but notice the lyrics all related to a lost sheep coming back to the fold. That is how it played, though it was somewhat surreal, as if I was observing this and not feeling it.

So on to Wednesday 23rd September 1981!!!

Out of the blue, something that had never happened before(!), I had an impromptu visit by my mum and my sisters whilst at work. And that very morning! (Unreal!)

I did not know how to feel. They knew nothing of what had happened and what was transpiring. Another surreal moment: like observing someone else greeting his own relatives.

Then the staff at work all kept looking my way, through the day, to see what would happen. Waiting on me to give them some news perhaps? Was this family visit connected? In the previous week, as well as the earlier sharing I mentioned, another rare event had happened. A customer had come in to the Workshop Reception with a box of chocolates. They stipulated that they wanted to thank me by name for work on their car. I made use of that to share it with all at work and add how to me it was like a last thing to share with them all (in anticipation for the great day)!

It may be, some expected me to come up with news of something like my having inherited a huge sum or been offered a prime job somewhere. I don't know (?).

Along with the warning the night before, I became conscious that two different threads of thoughts and impressions had in these last days been in parallel play in my mind. This had played out with my sharing of things. I was either peacefully sharing about the Lord or I was sharing about this "great event" and *that* sharing had a pressure, more forceful "I must share this" element. One repeating impression I had related to this great event, with a sense of urgency tension, whilst the other was more calm and about every day normality. For example there was a pull on me – an urge – to go and turn up in the lunchtime to a shop in the centre of town where

I hadn't been for a time. This was a small car parts and accessory place in a side street. I also had been reminded of my commitment as a child to sacrifice myself to a lion. How much more, surely, I should be ready and willing to give up my life for the sake of Jesus: for the gospel?

Then, there was this other thread: a calm thinking that recognised I actually had no reason to step out of my normal lunchtime routine. I had no need to have anything to do with that shop lunchtime. I resolved to live in the moment and not do anything that naturally was not called on me to do: not step out of the norm. This did not cease the tension straight away, but in the resolve, in the fact that it made sense, it was enough to prevent me change my routine: Not to go with the urge – or any urge, as I was now cautious – but instead to consciously move and act out step by step what was my normal lunchtime routine no matter what for this Wednesday.

Come the lunchtime, for which I had an hour, I went home as normal, where Sheila had left something for me to warm up to eat – my only hot meal of the day – as evenings were about coming home, have a shower, then dash up to Shalom for the evening's car jobs. So, though I had this urge again to go into town, since I had resolved not to do anything different, and since there was no natural business for me to be in town, I remained home. I retained my resolve for the duration of that lunchtime. It was a weird kind of feeling – that I should be somewhere else – but had no reason to be. But this resolve to not step out of the norm and not disturb the natural course of events was fortified by the news the night before of a "seducing spirit" which I was conscious of the possibility. If as yet, right then, I had little clue of what this fully meant. But it helped in my resolve. I did not go with the urge. I had my lunch, stayed in, then returned to work.

In the following days and weeks I learned that one of the guys at work had been involved in a knife fight at some time in his past (if I recall accurately). He certainly had been involved in a violent incident. And, I had noticed if pressed, could suddenly turn angry. It turns out that he had gone to that side street shop in the Wednesday lunchtime on the 23rd September. He also was one of the few guys at work with whom I had not yet witnessed.

Caffyns had two garages in Sevenoaks when I joined them after college. One was in the High Street at the top of the town which is where I began work with them and one was at *Tubs Hill* at the bottom of the hill near the railway station and behind a Shell petrol set of pumps. *Tubs Hill* was our Rolls Royce maintenance garage. We joked with those brown overall shod mechanics that they were our commercial vehicle division (The Rollers being the heavier cars). Then, a few hundreds yards further on the opposite side of the road and to the right, was a car dealership and garage which was then also purchased by *Caffyns*. This last place being the bigger site, the decision was made to combine all three service facilities under one roof. The High Street and *Tubs Hill* sites were then sold off. This last place near the "new" Police Station (of the time) is in 2017 the site of a big *Lidl* Supermarket. The situation meant that as the events above unfolded, the three different groups of mechanics were still integrating on the new site. This violent guy whom I hardly knew at that point had worked for the previous car dealership. And, as yet, the opportunity to tell him about the Lord had not yet materialised. Had I met him in the town outside of work, I would have tried to share with him. As it was, several weeks down the road from the fateful Wednesday, we did talk at work and got on okay. In a place with many mechanics, it doesn't take long for mutual respect in recognition of the knowledge and capabilities each have and expertise. Anyone unable to do their job proficiently is easily recognised. But, on that fateful Wednesday, with the final element of my presence there also being in place it looks like a violent scenario had been possible. I did not go and so, that did not happen, I did not die that day.

At the next Sunday gathering or within a few days I remember a clear word of interpretation or prophecy where the Lord said "I have much work for you to do". Another one in that time which fitted well with my throwing off the surplus of life and a focus on the essential was "Live each day as if it were your last". And, in my newish habit of going out for a walk and pray in the middle of the night, somewhere in or near Knole Park, I then said to the Lord something like this, "Lord, if you are going to let me live, then use my life to bring the maximum number of people to come to know Jesus". Little did I know how this would then set the tone for many years to come.

The night time walks began like this. At fourteen when I converted from agnosticism to follow Jesus my initial habit of devotion involved a daily time of prayer and a bible read on my knees by my bedside. Then, when I began work on cars and also in late evenings, whenever I would try and pray on my knees, I would regularly wake up hours later and realise I had fallen asleep (again). I would then get undressed and go to bed. This led me to a crisis internally as I found myself unable to cope well without being filled anew with the Holy Spirit. I needed this time alone with my God. But I kept falling asleep. And since that had been on my knees, it got to a point where I could not go on my knees anymore. They hurt and ached from having fallen asleep on them so often. So one day I was unusually free from "emergency" evening work (which is how many of the car jobs were handled). And, this being a bible study evening night – another at Fiona's home as it happens – I decided to go there on foot and talk to the Lord en route: I explained how I missed my times with him and did not know what to do as I was so tired and fell asleep on my knees, and now they hurt so much, I felt like I could not spend time with him: Help!

Well, as I walked past *The Vine*, the Lord, in a still small voice, clearly spoke three words: "Sit, Walk, Stand". Wow! Of course: Such simple wisdom. I did not have to be on my knees for this activity. Just as I was doing right then, walking and talking with him, I could do that regularly. Then, I suddenly remembered those three words, were also the title of a book I had known about. There was a book named *Sit, Walk, Stand* written by a gentleman called *Watchman Nee*. I then burst out laughing. I realised that the Lord had not only given me a word of wisdom in my situation, but had also just shared a joke with me. This book was written by "Watch Ma knee"!

So, at some part of 1981, as I was too tired to pray or read, I decided to begin a practise of getting up in the middle of the night. Then, I would get dressed and go for a walk and spend time with my God. This coincided with my having broken my alarm clock. And so to get to work on time in the morning, I asked the Lord to wake me up on time. I figured, if this failed at the first attempt, then I'd have to get a new alarm clock and apologise for my lateness. But, it was not needed. The Lord was faithful and for many years after that I no longer used an alarm clock, but asked the Lord instead. It was not long before I made a deal with the Lord for my "quiet times". If he woke me, I'd go and pray. It was up to Him to wake me; it was up to me to get up. And, I later added that if he awoke me between certain times I would do a longer walk. If He woke me before or after that time, that would mean a shorter route. Thus began a life of challenging and interesting intercession: of standing in the gap for various things, individuals and nations. So it was on such a night that in late September 1981 I prayed that prayer of commitment relating to revival. Keith and Sheila whose fellowship home I shared with their two boys, Jonathan and Luke knew nothing of these night walks. As far as I'm aware that is true. I kept asking the Lord to protect our times together and help me quietly leave and return. This practice made a significant difference to my progress and effectiveness daily. I noticed not a few things happen to others too. I especially love to hear the news of how this has helped others or how the paths of nations have changed as a result of this standing in the gap. But, as the importance of intercession is not the topic here, let's return to the matter of deception.

The series of coincidences, words, events, bible texts and various feelings and impressions that, all together, had led me to believe something was real or of God, and yet was not, they began to happen again, involving new subjects and new decisions. They had not ceased. I realised this deceiving spirit was still there! The spirit had not left. He had just gone on to attempt to make me believe new stories and new things as of God, or true, when they were not. This then began for me a very challenging and lonely time: A time of learning, figuring things out, searching, imploring the Lord in order to discern and understand: what was the Lord and what was this deceiving spirit? How could I tell? What were the fruits? It was a lonely time as I could share this with no one without being a cause of *their* confusion and a burden *to them* too. Charles it seems was avoiding me. I had to learn this! How to discern?

And, as I learned it became a real fight to take control. To take captive thoughts and imaginations and throw them down as required (2 Corinthians 10:5). And, step by step, as I fought and learned and resisted the voices and impressions, I became free. Overcoming deception – fighting deceiving spirits – is not about casting them out, but removing their hold on you. It is by re-learning the truth. But, it is not just about education per se, but about a true hungering and seeking after truth more than anything. Without a genuine desire for truth, no amount of education can help. We all see what we want to see, so only a true hunger for truth can lead into all truth, and *then* set us free. Doctors, scientists and other learned people also make up the membership of cults: education helps, but it is *not* the spiritual root of the matter.

There was something else that needed handling. At first I did not see it. But it became apparent, life in me died or was doing so. This gradually began to dawn on me. Having learned that the Lord had, in some way, been involved with an evil spirit directly, something in me had shut down. As that as yet, not understandable belief, of a flaw or error in God and his character became a new fact in my life, a darkness inside grew. It was perhaps the most empty time of my life. A void had formed. It was the very darkest time of my life. I had honestly and simply felt unable to doubt that God was all good. The fruits of this new (un-)belief was an emptiness which, only just by a simple surreal observation, became clearly evident one day. I was looking at a beautiful bouquet of flowers. And, as I did so, my observed thoughts made a connection to the intellectual recognition that I felt nothing. I felt utterly empty and devoid of feeling of any appreciation, of life, or of enjoyment as I recognised in my memory here was something known as beauty in front of me, but somehow I was not feeling it. I was totally devoid of feeling this. I recognised in these thoughts I was an alien in my own body. This was not like when someone is not in touch with their emotions. This was deeper than that. It was a spiritual and a mental non appreciation that here was beauty that I should be seeing, but I was not. I could not. So by faith alone, as I could still trust the Lord, whilst in this spiritual dark hole, I asked for His help. I was honest and said how I felt and that this should not be and, help! He began to speak through the gifts of the Spirit in the meetings and say things like "Only good comes from me". I believe he needed to repeat that. I think he said it at least twice over a period. I heard the words, realised they were from the Lord and must be true, but I could not feel them to be true. This truth directly spoke to me into the lie that God's involvement, His making use of a deceiving or lying spirit (cf. 1 Kings 22:19-23), meant that God himself was evil or acquainted with evil.

This is perhaps the first lie the enemy wanted Eve to believe (Genesis 3:1): "**Has God . . . said**"? You can't really trust God to be true (can you?).

The numbness, the emptiness and darkness inside had come out of believing God was directly involved with evil. It had occurred from believing that evil in some way came from Him. So when he said "Only good comes from me", this I had to make a choice about to believe. Faith at its root is a choice. It is a decision. I took it. I made it. I chose to believe this was true, even if I did not feel it was true, because of my specific experience. I did it, even though I did not understand. The understanding was to follow. And life in me began to return. Later on, this led me to recognise what John wrote as one of the most simple, but profound truth about God "**God is light and**

in Him is no darkness at all" (1 John 1:5). Emotionally this was settled in me years later by the vivid descriptions I read in George Ritchie's book *Return from tomorrow* in which I found a good and healthy glimpse of the genuine extent of the purity of God's love in the middle of what George experienced. I highly recommend George's book.

And one other thing reared it's head that I also needed to handle. This is as a result of what the Lord began to do publicly, since I had passed his test. I had come to realise that just as Abraham had been tested in offering Isaac, so my willingness to die was a test accomplished. Just as with Abraham God had a need to know something more as seen when He says "**now I know**" (Genesis 22:12; He did this with King Hezekiah too since we read "**. . . that He might know all *that was* in his heart.**" – 2 Chronicles 32:31) and then we read, as a direct result of this obedience, Abraham was blessed onwards (Genesis 22:15-18).

So, following that late September day, things changed with my participation in meetings. It was as if God *now* trusted me. From that point on, in a bible and sharing night, when I perceived what I thought the Lord was saying, and I shared it out loud, when it came to the time of the gifts, time and again the Lord spoke and, word for word literally repeated things I had shared, confirming me (cf. Isaiah 44:26). This began to happen immediately after that fateful day. It was a mixed blessing as I also had spiritual pride to counter. But it also helped to make sense of why God had directly been involved in testing me. In any event, perhaps to assist in my struggle with pride – well, at least it certainly helped put it in check – within a short space of time through the gifts, he began to confirm one or two others in exactly the same way word for word. It was kind of frightening and daunting at the same time and fostered a new sense of awe in the midst of the meetings/the fellowship – but this happened only for the few weeks up to the ending of the fellowship: from late September 81 to the Spring of 82.

No sooner had I begun to discern and differentiate between the Lord's voice and that of the deceiving spirit that 1982 – a new year – had begun. Within weeks some new "words" and a change in the normal routine of things in the fellowship became apparent. Words like "Each of you are a precious jewel in my crown" and "Remember the good things" and (I'm not sure about the accuracy of this next one, but it fits in well) "Fear not for what's ahead, for I am with you". Then, suddenly, in the Spring of 1982 Charles calls for an extraordinary meeting of all involved with the fellowship. I am asked to go and pick Peter up, but told not to collect the organ. We all meet up at the *Dunton Green Village Hall* mid week (if I recall – we'd never done that before) and, right there, all the Oxford, the Reading, the Streatham and the Tonbridge folk were there too: everyone possibly connected to the fellowship. Further, as we drove there, out of the blue, I develop a sore throat and find myself unable to speak out loud *at all*. We were seated differently than normal with Charles more in the centre of the room along one of the walls as opposed to one end of the building. Everyone else is in a semi circle type layout facing him. No musical instruments have been brought. Charles begins to share the news that since Ken's death the previous Spring news had emerged of things he would like to tell us all about. Ken in his final years had been involved with a number of women and there had even been an abortion. Shock! Disbelief! With this utterly stunning news a mixture of responses occurred. Conscious of my throat I could say nothing and, if things weren't strange enough already, as I was listening to Charles, somehow, I was not shocked [unlike most it seemed]. Instead I had a calm realisation which came out of the deep personal struggles I had been through. Having fought to know and recognise what was true and what was not. Because of the deceiving spirit experience, I now realised something. I had already experienced the trauma and the confusing time others were now beginning to enter into or about to experience.

But, what I now realised was: We had all been under a deceiving spirit/s.

Reflecting on the preceding 12 months I also recognised that, had I not been through my own personal struggle and fight with regards to truth versus error and *then* still heard this devastating news, I might have gone crazy or worse. I would have realised my total dedication to this man of God was betrayed and I was likely unable to have coped with it. Instead, because of what I'd experienced, I wanted to tell everybody of what I'd been through and help them with this news. It was not to be. In fact, now I'm glad I was prevented with the sore throat. I had not learned enough to communicate effectively. In the grief and shock of the news, any addition on my part may even have caused more hurt and pain in the midst of a confusing time. As it was, this news was already far *too much* for not a few. Some went on never to go to a church again or have anything to do with God. Some were never to be heard from or seen again. At the very least, the fellowship never met again.

I returned Peter to his home and, as I drove away from *Dunton Green* I realised my throat was quickly okay again. I could speak.

What struck me the most – rather than the news of betrayal or Ken's wrongdoing as was foremost on everybody else's mind – was that we had all been under the influence of deceiving spirits. I had not been alone. But, where perhaps I was alone, is in experiencing the fight to recognise and overcome the deceits as they are presented to our minds. Who else was recognising and understanding how that should be done?

The nearest I've come across from anyone to directly teach in this and similar to what I've experienced, is from the now late John Barr, an Elim Minister who had been involved in deliverance ministry for 30-40 years. I first dedicated to him my article *Wolf in sheep's clothing?* We met up in the later 80s – and the reader may have noted this book is dedicated to his memory. As I considered the time in the old fellowship I prayed to learn what were the tell tale signs in the group that indicate it was going astray: What are the kind of things to look out for while you are in the very midst of a group? What were the fruits to be seen to recognise the enemy has access to a group of believers? That is how I came to write *Wolf in sheep's clothing?*

And it is a later chapter in this book.

That such deception as I'd experienced was in fact the norm for whole chunks of Christendom was also a real eye opener. The truth that divisions of the Church, maintained for centuries or millennia had begun and were being retained by the direct intervention and "servicing" of deceiving spirits, this is a revelation to be grasped…

But before I share more I wish to provide a biblical discussion that demonstrates the normality of the spiritual world as I have experienced. I have entitled it *Which s/Spirit are you listening to?*

It is separately published as an article online and it is a needful separate chapter in my second book (chronologically) *Leadership is male?* The whole issue of Paul's writings relating to the role of women primarily involves how deception works differently with women than men and, without that particular appreciation seriously grasped, sadly, no work on this writing of Paul can help but really miss what he was on about.

I then will share the article I mentioned as dedicated to John Barr *Wolf in sheep's clothing?*

But, first I'd like to highlight the kind of things that charaterize the work of deceiving spirits.

THE CHARACTERISTICS OF DECEPTION

The following are various thoughts which help to identify the work of deceiving spirits in an individual's life or grouping. It is aimed as a help to leaders, counsellors and individuals desiring to help others or themselves to identify a direct work of deceiving spirits.

The Lord clearly warned as the major thing to look out for prior to his return "**take heed that no one deceives you**" Matthew 24:4, 11, 23-26 et al. And Paul made clear that in the latter times believers would give heed to "**deceiving spirits and doctrines of demons**" 1 Timothy 4:1

These spirits "teach" by stringing together many passages taken out of context (just as the Devil did when tempting Jesus: using only a portion of a text; Matthew 4:3-11). The way they "teach" is what I wish to highlight. These are not exhaustive, but indicative guidelines or signposts to show the difference between what is of God and what is not: how to identify the work of deceiving spirits.

Regularly or repeatedly occurring coincidences or, similar type events which act as a support to a belief, these are the work of deceiving spirits.

Facial feelings associated or timed with these incidents are the work of deceiving spirits.

Passages of scripture received as needed to "confirm" a thought or belief, but which are "received" by an opening of the Bible by coincidence at the right place and eyes or finger at the exact point required, are the work of deceiving spirits: This is so when repeatedly occurring. These will often be texts out of context – unrelated to the surrounding passage from which it is taken. These are not usually texts out of knowledge previously gained.

When you get these beliefs you either don't feel secure sharing them or, you feel they "must" be told (e.g. a persistent "hobby horse"). And *you* are "called" and it is "your duty": you "MUST" share these! The Lord has self control – a facet of the fruit of the Spirit (Galatians 5:22-23) – so, He leaves you with a choice; the enemy, the deceiving spirit has no patience: you are "obligated" to share.

If the former (feeling) where you don't feel secure sharing them: the belief is felt as "personal" and "special" such that you end up being extra careful who you share these beliefs with and to the full: Certainly not sharing these with someone who does not fully affirm you (already), and not without much explanation – disguise – covering remarks to justify. Associated and together with this is the idea that one has an "exclusive".

Classic Fruits of Deception

Basically here *isolation* and *exclusivity* are classic fruits of deception as are *domination, control,* and *repeated accusation of the brethren* to any degree (that is to say other brethren not in your group). The latter signs are more visible and tangible in a group of believers under deception. An individual feels especially guarded about his belief being attacked and has difficulty in accepting others who do not share the same belief. They find it hard to remain with and accept the freedom of the other to believe otherwise. Which is against 1 Corinthians 13:7 where love "**. . . believes all things . . .**" and James 3:17 where God's wisdom is "**. . . willing to yield . . .**" and, 2 Corinthians 3:17 "**. . . where the Spirit of the Lord is, there is liberty**", freedom. It is the freedom of the other to believe otherwise which is not "given" permission.

The feeling that if one should dare to doubt or question this "belief" one will lose something: Whilst the opposite is true with things from God because he gives a genuine choice and does not need to impose his truth. It speaks for itself.

Deception is, believing something is of God with sincerity and usually with no doubt, whilst in fact it is not wholly or at all of God.

Paul sincerely believed the followers of "the way" (the 1st Christians – Acts 19:23) were corrupting the truths of the religion of the One and True God. This is why he persecuted them vehemently and was able to say later, after his conversion "**I have lived in all good conscience before God until this day**" (Acts 23:1). Once he had learned "the way" was the real truth and not a false belief as he thought, he could not persecute, but sought to re-align all his knowledge of the Word to this "way" (Acts 9:1-19 cf. 1 Timothy 1:12-13).

When a Bible passage is repeatedly brought to the mind and this is linked to a belief such that it demands an action on your behalf (due to the repetition) to make something happen, then this is the work of deceiving spirits:

For example being repeatedly told "**faith without works is dead**", "**faith without works is dead**", "**faith without works is dead**", when linked to a belief having been introduced by the spirit about someone which is to be "your" partner. [James 2:20]

Another example is repeatedly being given "they will know that a prophet has been among them" linked to a "teaching" absorbed, "requiring" you to share it no matter how offensive or inappropriate or untimely or unwelcome (because, " 'you' are a prophet!"). [Ezekiel 2:5]

It must not be forgotten that with the Lord and his words: "**the spirits of the prophets are subject to the prophets**" 1 Corinthians 14:32.

"Compulsion", "pressure" to act or speak, to initiate or continue a change in lifestyle, in your job, in a relationship, etc are not God's methods.

Jesus leads his sheep; he does not "drive" them.

Because they hear his voice (John 10:4)

Those who "**are led by the Spirit of God, these are sons of God**" (Romans 8:14). God has self-control (Galatians 5:23); the enemy does not, but seeks to impose his will.

As I have shared, a lonely heart is particularly fertile ground for a work of deception. The path to believing someone is to be "your" partner well frequented by such spiritual activity. Once deceiving spirits have a hold – once you are believing something "received" – they will feed it and lead it on to other areas of control in your life in order to isolate you. The thief comes to steal, kill, and destroy any part of the abundant life God has for you (John 10:10). He attempts to blind you to the truth by veiling your eyes – the Bible becomes a hard book to read – anointed teaching is dull to your ears…

May the above few thoughts help you in your walk with the Lord and in your ministry.

I leave you with A PRAYER which is a good beginning to allow one's heart attitude to receive freedom and understanding:

Dear Father,

Thank you that you are Light and in you is no darkness at all.

I ask that you shine your light in me and reveal all the beliefs and thoughts which I have taken on board as if from you, but in reality are not of you. I want to believe what is from you and nothing from the enemy. Just as you asked the church at Laodicea to anoint their eyes with eye salve that they may see, so I ask that you anoint my eyes that I may see. I thank you that the Holy Spirit will guide into all truth. I ask for discernment and courage to unlearn wrong things received as well as prevent new things which attempt to make a home in me. Help me to recognise any fresh work of the enemy which attempts to divert me from your ways.

Thank you that you give wisdom freely to those who ask.

Father I ask all this in Jesus' Name,

Amen

(1 John 1:5; Revelation 3:18; John 16:13;
James 1:5-8; John 16:23)

WHICH s/SPIRIT ARE YOU LISTENING TO?

We are told by John:

> . . . test the spirits . . .
>
> *1 John 4:1*

This is a chapter about the need to do that and how.

This helps solidify much of what has preceded with the bible: To show in scripture the reality of the enemy's activity in the life of the believer.

But before I go there I will split hairs. When I say *Which s/Spirit are you listening to?* it could be understood, don't listen or, do not hear, but what I am after explaining is, don't go on to obey the voice of the enemy. And by the enemy of course I am referring to demons or evil spirits: whichever you prefer to call them. It is okay to hear them; not to heed them.

I will explain how it is okay to hear them. We know that in the wilderness Satan tempted Jesus:

> . . . Jesus was led up by the Spirit into the wilderness to be tempted by the devil.
>
> *Matthew 4:1*

So from this we know two important things relevant to this discussion. One is that it is not bad to hear (listen in that sense) the enemy speaking to you. And second, if Jesus was talked to by the enemy then we should expect it too. It is what you do with what he (the enemy) says, that is important.

In the Christian life and even more so, in the Spirit filled Christian life, sensitivity to the spiritual is heightened. By Spirit filled I am referring to the baptism in the Holy Spirit and I have written separately about that in my article *What is Baptism in the Holy Spirit?* (Free to read at jarom.net)

This increased access to spiritual things to the mind of a person causes a greater hearing of things: both from the Lord and from the enemy. What tends to happen is without discernment the enemy is often mistaken to be the Lord speaking and thus the person will get involved in (sometimes) good things at the expense of the best. Or, the person is made to do something ahead of a proper "natural" time. That is very common. Let alone all the other more usual stuff from the enemy like enticement to sin or influence to believe false doctrine (1 Timothy 4:1). Or, worry attacks, fear attacks leading to panics and anxiety, guilt attacks leading to condemnation, etc…

So does the enemy speak often to us?

Often is misleading, regularly is more accurate: Yes, I believe so. When Jesus was tempted in the desert as mentioned above this was a one off special occasion, but we are then told:

> **And when the devil had ended all the temptation, he departed from him for a season.**
>
> *Luke 4:13 KJV*

This was one season only. But, there were more. Indeed when Peter spoke to Jesus and against what He had just been explaining, Jesus perceived the enemy at work and so, He said,

> **Get behind Me, Satan! You are an offense to Me, for you are
> not mindful of the things of God, but the things of men.**
>
> *Matthew 16:23*

Jesus knew how to test the spirits and only just a few moments after complimenting Peter on hearing from the Father (Matthew 16:17), He now instead told him off for uttering from another spirit. James tells us how to respond to the enemy's voice:

> **Therefore submit to God. Resist the devil and he will flee
> from you.**
>
> *James 4:7*

When you resist the enemy, you are refusing to accept what he says, he then flees. But, don't be fooled into thinking he is gone for good. It will only be the current season in which you have fought that he flees from. Jesus said,

> **A disciple is not above *his* teacher, nor a servant above
> his master.**
>
> *Matthew 10:24*

Of course this is a reference to persecution and the fact that what Jesus endured we are not to expect to be exempt from. But I believe as the above passages show that this is also true of the enemy's access to us when he attempts to influence us: his speaking in order to divert us from God and His ways. He tried it with Jesus and he tries it on with us. So our job is as Paul put it, to be:

> **. . . bringing every thought into captivity to the obedience
> of Christ.**
>
> *2 Corinthians 10:5*

The enemy speaks to us just like the Lord through the means of our thought life. To our minds, through dreams sometimes and, through other's words: as the example with Peter and Jesus above. What Paul just wrote is good to help us see this is a spiritual battlefield involving the mind:

> **For the weapons of our warfare *are* not carnal but mighty in God for pulling down strongholds, casting down arguments and every high thing that exalts itself against the knowledge of God, bringing every thought captive to the obedience of Christ . . .**
>
> ### *2 Corinthians 10:4-5*

It is the thought life that is the battleground. And it is our responsibility to take captive every thought not in line with Jesus.

The challenge

Once it is recognised that the enemy is involved in this activity of feeding the thought life, then the practise is to go against what he says.

So, the remaining issue now is one of discernment. How do you recognise it is the enemy, or the Lord, or just your very own thoughts?

These are the three main activities prevalent in the mind. How can you tell which is whose?

If the hurdle is passed that the enemy does regularly have an input in the lives of Christians, just as he did with Jesus: it happens regularly to all Christians, then the remaining issue is to discern the voices and then heed the good one and resist the bad one: Knowing how to deal with these things. So as John put it we need to:

. . . test the spirits . . .

1 John 4:1

The simplest and easiest way is to know what is being said and line it up with what is known as right and wrong. If the feeling is of hate and desire to murder, then of course that is wrong and needs to be resisted. That is the means to kick out such a feeling. By resisting it and deciding that is not what you want in your life. This is effectively what the Lord told Cain right at the beginning:

> **If you do well, will you not be accepted? And if you do not do well, sin lies at the door. And it's desire *is* for you, but you should rule over it.**
>
> *Genesis 4:7*

By resisting the sin's call to act you disarm its hold on you. It is of note that sin is personified in what the Lord said to Cain. My understanding of this is more in terms of evil spirits identifying with a particular sinful activity than the deed itself being a type of person. Either way, it is resisting the feeling, the urge, the overriding influence or pressure to do evil which is the crux. But, conversely by heeding it you are less able to overcome later as you have welcomed it. It thereby begins to make a home in you. However, your ability to return or resist is never removed fully: it may be hidden and quenched as Paul said, but it is always there to some extent. Paul spoke of this ability being severely hampered in terms of a conscience sealed up:

> **. . . having their own conscience seared with a hot iron . . .**
>
> *1 Timothy 4:2*

And Jesus spoke of what "one had" as being taken away. This signifies that "we all had it" in the first place. So our use of it enables our retention of it. I will need to expand on this: to explain it. Jesus said:

> **For whoever has, to him more will be given, and he will have abundance; but whoever does not have, even what he has will be taken away from him.**
>
> *Matthew 13:12*

This is in fact a fundamental principle. So important, that Jesus is quoted 5 times as saying it in the gospels. But is it preached about? Is it understood? Not very much is the answer.

At first glance it appears unfair. If you have something more is given you, but if you have nothing what you do have is removed. But, this is not material things Jesus is referring to. It is a spiritual principle. And this principle – this law if you will – is important in establishing an effective means of discerning what the enemy says to you as a believer. Indeed deception, it is often thought, you should counteract just by education. This is not so. The most educated and wise people are amongst the deceived. This is because the enemy has been listened to and the matter is not just intellectual, but spiritual. The answer to deception is education with a right attitude of heart: with the right type of desire for truth in the heart. Education on its own is not the answer.

So what is Jesus referring to?

He is referring to the desire in the heart to do what is right, to sincerely knowing the truth, to truly love God. If you have this, then more ability will be given you and you will have abundance. But, if you do not have pure motive in your heart, what you do have – even your very ability to choose – will appear unusable as you enter the realm of deception. It will still be with you – the freedom to choose – but your heart will cause you not to see, to be blinded thus and not able to choose the good from the bad. This is why Jesus taught in parables:

> *. . . Lest they should see with their eyes and hear with their ears, lest they should understand with their heart and turn, so that I should heal them.*
>
> *Matthew 13:15*

Jesus knew the ability remained, but because of their inner choice to not desire the truth: their motives being impure, in order to "respect that" freedom, He spoke in parables thus it was their own hearts that prevented them from understanding and turning. But, Jesus turned (in His speech) to His disciples and then said:

> **But blessed *are* your eyes for they see, and your ears for they hear...**
>
> *Matthew 13:16*

So the first step to effective discernment is having the right heart. This is why James started the mention of resisting the enemy with humbling yourself before God first.

> **Therefore submit to God. Resist the devil and he will flee from you.**
>
> *James 4:7*

If this is a regular practise in your daily life then, you are doing this first step anyway. If your daily habit is to spend time with your God, then you are in a place of humility before your God which is of value in this matter: If not all the way through your day, at the very least at that part of your day. This then enables the Lord to highlight what the enemy may have put your way. Your spirit may be spoken to by the Lord. At all times the enemy may speak, the Lord however is into having a relationship and as such needs to be invited, welcomed, asked; not assumed upon. He has self-control; the enemy does not. So that He will not always speak immediately into a situation if not asked.

> **. . . the fruit of the Spirit is love, joy, peace, longsuffering, kindness, goodness, faithfulness, gentleness, self-control . . .**
> **Galatians 5:22-23**

Not only is this useful to know about God – that He has self-control – and thus how important it is we spend time with Him, but it is a valuable aspect of recognising the enemy when he speaks. What the enemy says will not involve self-control on his part. He will pressure, cajole, squeeze, with a thought or feeling to get you to do or believe something. The Lord will not. The Lord instead returns to mention something again (though to a limited amount of times). This latter point is relevant in that if you do not want to hear Him, the Lord will also not go on.

Jesus leads His sheep; He does not "drive" them!

But His heart remains the same, so if you do seek His face you will find Him repeating what He may have said a long time ago.

> **. . . many are called, but few *have* mettle.**
> **Matthew 20:16 JM**

cf. *Deleting ELECT in the bible* – the Greek word EKLEKTOS means "excellent/top quality"

The call remains the same, but often the fulfilment does not occur or is not seen since the response to the call is down to the individual.

So pressure to do something which does not allow for your choice is invariably the enemy trying to influence you. If he can't wait for a day to do this thing, then it is not normally the Lord. This is the spirit of the voice I am talking about: A regular facet of the enemy's ways. But the Lord does at times require us to act quickly and do something within a brief time frame. Usually in these times it is our personal fear or laziness that prevents us to act. It normally involves our conscience and thus is God's speaking revealed. The enemy does not use the conscience; he uses guilt. There is a difference.

These are useful aspects to know when trying to recognise what is going on in our minds, our hearts, our feelings… Sometimes these things are too strong, or they feel that way. But, if in doubt just say, "Lord. I am not sure this is you, I will wait a while". He will understand. If it is Him, He will then open your mind to a passage of the bible or something that will encourage you to understand this is Him. If not, anything the enemy gives extra will also with it have a "pressure" indicator. You must because it needs to happen now to prove things, etc…

It is the opposite with the Lord because,

> **…where the Spirit of the Lord *is*, there is liberty.**
>
> **2 Corinthians 3:17**

There is freedom, release where Jesus is. There is peace and He is gentle.

So the thought, the word or suggestion received can be discerned as to what source, what spirit is speaking by the tone and manner of voice. It is the fruit of the voice that tells us the source. Pressure, compulsion is the enemy's; conviction, gentle persuasion is the Lord's.

The important thing is to sincerely desire righteousness, talk to God with absolute honesty with Him and yourself, asking for His help and then watch for the tell-tale pressure or the simple conviction and inspiration. If in doubt wait, quieten your heart and soon the tone will tell the source. But, don't be fooled in thinking the enemy never speaks. He does regularly. But so does the Lord.

A powerful weapon

Just as Jesus used the Scripture to respond to the Devil in the wilderness, so the bible is like a sword and is most effective in resisting the enemy once he is recognised as speaking or trying to influence. If you do not know a scripture to "speak into" your current situation ask the Lord for one. How you receive that is also important to recognise. The enemy loves to string passages together – usually out of context – to "convince" the person of his cause. I recommend my earlier chapter *The Characteristics of deception* to help in recognising that type of scripture giving. If you have been following such a "string" of passages for some time and do not know it, you may find my later chapter *Making an idol* useful in recognising such. I will leave you here with a verse that I have often found helpful to fight with:

> . . . seek first the kingdom of God and His righteousness, and all these things shall be added to you.
>
> **Matthew 6:33**

Now, for some basic attitudes of heart that don't just help, but are essential in overcoming deception: I entitle this chapter *Overcoming Deception.*

OVERCOMING DECEPTION

Let's recap:

What is deception?

It is believing something that is not true. That perhaps would be one of the simplest definitions. More specific it is sincerely believing something as absolutely true or real or good or truly of God when it is not so.

What I wish to address is how to overcome the work of deceiving spirits.

Deception is more than just holding to a fable or general folklore like Santa or the tooth fairy. It is being given an idea or thought which because of the source of that concept – a deceiving spirit – the influence to believe that thing is real on the person and, once chosen, it is then regularly fed and affirmed by that spirit, to ensure faithfulness, but more so as a type of regular due. It is never enough for a demon to have obtained a hold or an opening in someone's life. They need to receive regular adulation and worship. To do this they make the "believer" aware of reminders or new facets or any means that help affirm the "belief". It is powerful stuff.

I explained some of the ways deceiving spirits "teach" in the earlier chapter *The characteristics of deception*. Another helpful chapter which laid down the need to discern what is received is *Which s/Spirit are you listening to?*

That deceiving spirits exist and are to be dealt with can be seen in what Paul wrote:

> **Now the Spirit expressly says that in latter times some will depart from the faith, giving heed to deceiving spirits and doctrines of demons,**
>
> *1 Timothy 4:1*

A good first step to overcome is to know these spirits exist and how they operate. This is because if you recognise you have come to believe something and, you know of such activity as described is what you experienced to lead you to believe, then you are already equipped to begin to overcome. If you do not know there is a problem, then you never have to think about dealing with that problem. But if you begin to question the means which were present to initiate the belief, then you begin to see the challenge.

Teachable not gullible

The enemy works on the level of co-operation with the flesh and in league with other fallen spirits. Pride is one of the best holds the enemy has on people. Another issue of great effect is any feeling held against another. Both of these, pride and our attitude towards others, involve superiority over others and as such reduces the ability to hear and receive truth that is present to set us free. Both these hindrances can be seen as follows:

Pride

> **But He gives more grace. Therefore He says: "*God resists the proud, but gives grace to the humble.*" Therefore submit to**

> **God. Resist the devil and he will flee from you. Draw near to God and He will draw near to you. Cleanse *your* hands, *you* sinners; and purify *your* hearts, *you* double-minded.**
>
> ***James 4:6-8***

When you are proud you cut yourself off from the source of life and light. God resists you and as He is the Truth, pride prevents you accessing it. For more help to recognise if pride might be in your heart I recommend my later chapter *Pride is a killer*. I have placed it after the following one entitled *Making an idol*.

Attitude towards others

> **He who loves his brother abides in the light, and there is no cause for stumbling in him. But he who hates his brother is in darkness and walks in darkness, and does not know where he is going, because the darkness has blinded his eyes.**
>
> ***1 John 2:10-11***

God is love is not some airy fairy feeling or concept of a dream life or another existence; love is a hard fact of reality which, if not practised, totally prevents you to receive truth to guard your heart or to set you free. Only with love for others in your heart can you have *nothing* to make you stumble.

> **Beloved, let us love one another, for love is of God; and everyone who loves is born of God and knows God. He who does not love does not know God, for God is love.**
>
> ***1 John 4:7-8***

Both in regards to pride and attitude towards others what is of note for overcoming deception is that *it is not intelligence and knowledge that are most important.* Good teaching is great, but no amount of knowledge beats love for overcoming deception. This is because:

> **. . . Knowledge puffs up, but love edifies.**
>
> *1 Corinthians 8:1*

If you want to have access to truth to be set free by, then good teaching is discernible by love of others that makes you a listener: with such God shares easily.

A good test to know if your belief system has become the wisdom justified of her children (Matthew 11:19) is to see how you hold it in regards to others. I give examples of this in the following chapter *Making an idol.*

The Scripture versus what you believe

The only root source for doctrine for a Christian is the Bible. Paul wrote:

> **All Scripture *is* given by inspiration of God, and *is* profitable for doctrine, for reproof, for correction, for instruction in righteousness,**
>
> *2 Timothy 3:16*

All Scripture: not just the didactic, but the narrative too, but everything in context. The enemy knows this so well that as explained in the other sections above his classic method of "teaching" is by stringing texts out of context together. Then he veils the mind to any part of a context that takes away from the use of the specific emphasis given to the element employed out of context: And then, constantly being legalistic about the words of that element: overemphasizing and repeating the facet used to deceive with.

Always hold the Scripture with higher regard to a system of belief you currently hold. This is what the Bereans did and why they were so highly commended by Paul.

> These were more fair-minded than those in Thessalonica, in that they received the word with all readiness, and searched the Scriptures daily *to find out* whether these things were so.
>
> *Acts 17:11*

But in all things, just as with prophecy, hold on to what is good:

> Test all things; hold fast what is good.
>
> *1 Thessalonians 5:21*

The Lord is THE Teacher

> . . . for One is your Teacher, the Christ . . .
>
> *Matthew 23:8*

> I will instruct you and teach you in the way you should go; I will guide you with My eye.
>
> *Psalm 32:8*

> If any of you lacks wisdom, let him ask of God, who gives to all liberally and without reproach, and it will be given to him.
>
> *James 1:5*

> But the anointing which you have received from Him abides
> in you, and you do not need that anyone teach you; but as
> the same anointing teaches you concerning all things, and
> is true, and is not a lie, and just as it has taught you, you will
> abide in Him.

> *1 John 2:27*

Note: There is a world of difference between any particular person (over others) to teach you which includes any certain group (over others) and – in contrast to – the need for the Body of Christ for teachers in general: there is a purpose in God's ongoing kingdom for apostles, prophets and teachers as the foundation continues to be laid on Christ by these (Ephesians 4:11; 2:20). But, if the enemy is claiming in your mind or, someone or, a particular group asserts, *they* are the only teacher or set of teachers to listen to, then 1 John 2:27 applies fully.

But seek with all your heart:

> And you will seek Me and find *Me*, when you search for Me
> with all your heart.

> *Jeremiah 29:13*

Keep asking questions. Keep re-evaluating. Be encouraged with,

> For whoever has, to him more will be given, and he will have
> abundance; but whoever does not have, even what he has
> will be taken away from him.

> *Matthew 13:12*

If you have a real desire for truth more will be given you; if your heart is not true in this, then deception has you.

MAKING AN IDOL?

What is an idol?

An idol is anything which is put in the place of God in your life. Particularly it is anything which you worship or spend much time thinking about. Inevitably it is something or someone which you would gladly talk about almost anytime.

The purpose of this section is to identify what an idol is and how to check if you have one. If you then find yourself as with an idol and you do not wish this, you can then begin to address that with help of a prayer at the end of this chapter.

An idol can be an object, a person, a teaching or idea or, anything which takes up the place of God. It is particularly relevant to believers as it is that which is placed before the God whom they know. For the Christian it is that which is put before God and His kingdom – His purposes. Jesus said:

> **If anyone comes to Me and does not hate his father and mother, wife and children, brothers and sisters, yes, and his own life also, he cannot be My disciple.**
>
> *Luke 14:26*

The moment you become a Christian you are in a warfare footing. You are in God's army and you have an enemy: the Devil and his minions. He knows that you become less effective for the Kingdom of God if you place anything as of greater value than God or, His purposes. And that is what happens on a regular basis if you have an idol.

This is so fundamental to the warfare believers are involved in that Satan has made available demons to deceive believers specifically in the area of idols. These will deceive believers to believe and to go on believing something is more important than God at any level. We know demons are directly involved where idols are concerned because Paul stated:

> **What am I saying then? That an idol is anything, or what is offered to idols is anything? But *I* say that the things which the Gentiles sacrifice they sacrifice to demons and not to God, and I do not want you to have fellowship with demons.**
>
> *1 Corinthians 10:19-20*

What are the effects of having an idol?

The attention and love you have for God and the attention and love you have for people is directly affected by an idol.

Because the idol is felt important it causes all contact with others who have stated otherwise – in regards to the idol – to be shunned or, looked down upon. They are the ones "missing out". Knowing this idol is more important than knowing those who do not think so. The way others are treated is a good indicator of having an idol.

Another good indicator of an idol is how captivated you are with Jesus, your Lord in worship. When in fellowship with other believers, during worship an idol will come to mind regularly. If, as mentioned above you are with others who do not see the importance you have for your idol, then in worship times another sign is to be conscious of those people and think of them as needing help – incomplete or, even harmful.

Why should these effects occur?

As the scripture above shows demons have a direct interest in idols. This being so they feed the mind with accusations about others. They remind the idol worshipper of the idol to take the place of the Lord in a worship time. They will direct the individual to the idol when insecurities are present.

As with any deception the classic fruits of the enemy's activity apply: *domination (control), isolation, exclusivity, accusing of the brethren*. With an idol this is in direct link to that idol. If the idol is a teaching or, an idea then, as Jesus stated:

> . . . wisdom is justified by all her children.
>
> *Luke 7:35*

In other words, the teaching even though it may be good in itself, it is held in higher esteem than the Lord or, the Kingdom. The teaching is not held as a tool for a job, but as the tool, the master, the answer. The believer acts as a child of the teaching. You don't hold it; it holds you.

The outworking of this is that if you are in leadership then anything the Lord wishes to do with someone else can be quenched or redirected in accord with the idol. Progress is made if the idol is given it's proper due. If someone has a call from the Lord to do something and there are steps towards that which are known, the idol is often imposed as needing to be addressed before this calling or these steps are freely permitted.

The teaching will be carried out regularly lest a lack of faithfulness to the idol is perceived. Shelves of this idea or teaching will be full of books prominently displayed. Preaching involves mentioning this idol regularly – often without fail – right down to including it or, making it the prominent theme in say, a wedding speech or sermon. Is this putting the couple first and that occasion?

Demons not only accuse the "unbeliever" in the mind of the idol worshipper, but they will where access is given, place or, impose whatever feelings they can on the "unbeliever" to make them bow to the "believer": Or, to seek help from the "believer" – the idol worshipper. The standing of the "unbeliever" in the minds of the "believer" is affected by the "taking on board" of the feelings as their own. These kinds of feelings can outwardly look very real and honest. But the "unbeliever" is actually not reacting out of himself or herself, but out of what is spiritually imposed. If the "unbeliever" truly submits to these then they become a "believer" in the minds of the idol worshipper and are "accepted". Lasting peace and security do not come from this however and further "bowing down" is felt as the way forward whilst in fact the opposite is true. Jesus alone is the source of peace.

A prayer

I have borrowed much of the prayer at the end of my earlier chapter *The Characteristics of Deception*.

If in reading you are already conscious of an idol then be honest with God and share this with Him. Turn from following this idol and instead hold it in its proper place. It may be valuable and important, but never as important as the Lord and His purposes. Ask for His help in this.

Dear Father,

Thank you that you are Light and in you is no darkness at all.

I ask that you shine your light in me and reveal all the beliefs and thoughts which I have taken on board as if from you, but in reality are not of you.

I want to believe what is from you and nothing from the enemy.

Just as you asked the church at Laodicea to anoint their eyes with eye salve that they may see, so I ask that you anoint my eyes that I may see.

I ask this as I may be blind to idols in my life and ask that you reveal them.

Show me where my worship to you is interfered by an idol.

Show me where my relationship with others are influenced by an idol.

I repent and reject all idols (name any here).

It is only you that I want as first in my life.

And it is you alone I wish to have as Lord.

Thank you that you promise to forgive all those who confess their sins to you.

I receive your forgiveness now.

Thank you.

I thank you that the Holy Spirit will guide into all truth.

I ask for discernment and courage to unlearn wrong things received as well as prevent new things which attempt to make a home in me.

Help me to recognise any fresh work of the enemy which attempts to divert me from your ways.

Thank you that you give wisdom freely to those who ask.

Father I ask all this in Jesus' Name,

Amen.

> (1 John 1:5; Revelation 3:18; John 16:13;
> James 1:5-8; John 16:23)

PRIDE IS A KILLER

Pride kills life. It will ruin your pleasure of someone else's company. It murders friendships and tarnishes relationships.

Embedded pride blinds the eyes and stops the ears and makes a way for destruction.

> **Pride *goes* before destruction, and a haughty spirit before a fall.**
>
> *Proverbs 16:18*

The shortened version "**Pride *goes* before . . . a fall**" misses the harder tone of the word "**destruction**".

Pride gives vent to presumptuous thought. Imagination let loose for self exaltation. The bible is full of reference to this kind of imagination out of an evil heart.

> **. . . proud in the imaginations of their hearts.**
>
> *Luke 1:51 (see Genesis 6:5, 8:21, Jeremiah 7:24, 23:17 et al)*

Fruit of pride

Pride always has an answer: There is nothing said to which it does not give a reply or judgment.

Pride always thinks it knows better – has heard it before – it is never wrong.

Pride changes its story to appear that it was not in error in the 1st place.

Pride blinds.

It kills your ability to hear God because,

God resists the proud, but gives grace to the humble.

James 4:6

So, how can we know we have pride if it makes us blind?

How can we realise its existence in us when we are blind to it?

I once asked the Lord that very question.

Why?

Because I had come to realise I was having a big problem with pride and it was dominating my life: Killing it.

It was a season which begun or accelerated a home for pride in me as a result of presumptuous thought. I had begun to believe in my own self importance.

Making a home for pride

In the late 1970s when in my late teens I was studying at a College of Further Education in Tonbridge a town in the South of England. The Course was for a Diploma in Automobile Engineering and Motor Retail Trade Management. At the same time we were covering Motor Vehicle Technicians and Crafts examinations with the City and Guilds Institutes of London: A 3 year deal. At the end of the 2nd year, Motor Vehicle

Technicians II and Crafts II exams were carried out and I recall praying for help (as one does).

I recall specifically asking for help in revising what was needed. On one occasion this led to revising exactly what was in an exam paper immediately before that very test.

So it should have been no surprise when the results came through later that year that "Distinction" was the mark given for those exams. It had been a partnership with the Lord in bringing about. That was fair enough until…

A few months later, the news filtered through that I had the best marks in the country for the Technicians Exam and the 2nd best marks in the Country for the Crafts!

This is rewarded by the issuing of Sterling Silver medals by the City and Guilds body in London.

Now soon after, I started thinking "Well just one exam fine, but TWO must (surely) mean I *must* have a certain ability above everybody else…''

That was a clear invitation for PRIDE as I came to believe that presumptuous thought.

But Ability is not Availability. My being available to God and His use of me does not reflect on my ability (or any greatness in me), but His faithfulness. No matter how able, it is your availability which God looks for. A heart attitude and a mind set to do God's will knowing that without God we can do nothing – John 15:5 "**without Me you can do nothing**" Jesus said.

So, having lived with pride and come to recognise (after a time) I had a problem with it, I prayed:

Lord, how can I know I have pride in my heart when it makes me blind to its very presence?

The answer

The Lord led me to read Psalm 34:1-3

> **I will bless the LORD at all times; His praise *shall* continually *be* in my mouth. My soul shall make its boast in the LORD; the humble shall hear *of it* and be glad. Oh, magnify the LORD with me, and let us exalt His name together.**
>
> *Psalm 34:1-3*

He then taught me from Verse 2

> **My soul shall makes its boast in the LORD; the humble shall hear *of it* and be glad.**
>
> *Psalm 34:2*

My attention was drawn to "**the humble shall hear *of it* and be glad**", that is to say, the proud shall hear and not be glad.

This got me interested.

What do the proud hear and are not glad about?

When someone shares about what the Lord has done for them (and it has nothing to do with me), if I am glad for them then I am not proud, but humble; When I am not glad, but listen with something else to add (to "their" story), then I am proud.

This opened my eyes to catching – to noticing – the existence of pride in my heart. By the act of seeing how I reacted to what others were sharing with me. By seeing the fruit of pride I could know of its existence: it's reality in my heart.

What to do

As I recognised I was not listening to others (listening "with them") I saw pride in my heart.

Then, while they were still talking I would cry in my heart to the Lord for help to *really* listen. I would make extra effort to concentrate on hearing the other person. As if the whole purpose of my existence at that moment was to listen and be there for that person.

Doing that set me on a path of overcoming pride. Sometimes I would confess "I am sorry, I did not hear properly, please say it again". I could bless the person with "That's great!", "Terrific!", "Well done!" and mean it, without adding any more (of myself – of my own judgment).

Other tools to help

You can also "catch" pride's presence by recognising presumptuous thoughts active in your mind: By noticing your imagination running loose. This is not the same as visualising or picturing something: being visionary, but thoughts based on self-exaltation.

Once recognised, just confess it to the Lord and move on. It is the essential and necessary work of,

> **. . . casting down arguments and every high thing that exalts itself against the knowledge of God, bringing every thought into captivity to the obedience of Christ.**
>
> **2 Corinthians 10:5**

Remember: it is not having the thoughts – the temptation – that makes you guilty, but holding on to them: the making them your own.

If the issue persists, then a great tool is fasting. I have found this useful especially if it persists immediately before a time of service or ministry in the midst of other folk – just to go without food with the intent of humbling my soul so I can hear God and be generally more effective/of use. David wrote,

. . . I humbled myself with fasting . . .

Psalm 35:13

So, are you listening and glad for your Brother or Sister's story?

O, to have your heart O God. A *"tender" "heart"*
(2 Chronicles 34:27 cf. Vss 18-28)

WOLF IN SHEEP'S CLOTHING?

How do you discern a wolf in sheep's clothing?

How can you tell someone who is leading others astray?

What are the signs?

Possible Answer: The miracles testify to the validity of the Man of God?

There are clear examples of miracles being a sign to vouch for the person as agent of these being someone the Lord is sending. Moses is a classic case in point:

> . . . the LORD said to him, "What *is* that in your hand?" And he said, "A rod." And He said, "Cast it on the ground." So he cast it on the ground, and it became a serpent; and Moses fled from it. Then the LORD said to Moses, "Reach out your hand and take *it* by the tail" (and he reached out his hand and caught it, and it became a rod in his hand), "that they may believe that the LORD God of their fathers, the God of Abraham, the God of Isaac, and the God of Jacob, has appeared to you."
>
> *Exodus 4:2-5*

Then there was the sign of his hand becoming leprous and being healed just by the act of placing it in and out of his cloak.

> **Then it will be, if they do not believe you, nor heed the message of the first sign, that they may believe the message of the latter sign.**
>
> *Exodus 4:8*

And thirdly there was the turning of water into blood (Exodus 4:6-9). Jesus and the apostles are also recorded as being recognised by the miracles. After Jesus had healed a man who had been infirm for 38 years He says of the Father (John 5:1-19):

> **. . . the Father loves the Son, and shows Him all things that He Himself does; and He will show Him greater works than these, that you may marvel.**
>
> *John 5:20*

This identifies the healing of the infirm as a "work" in Jesus' language. Such that when He says:

> **If I do not do the works of My Father, do not believe Me; but if I do, though you do not believe Me, believe the works, that you may know and believe that the Father *is* in Me, and I in Him.**
>
> *John 10:37-38*

> **Believe Me that I *am* in the Father and the Father in Me, or else believe Me for the sake of the works themselves. Most assuredly, I say to you, he who believes in Me, the works that I do he will do also; and greater *works* than these he will do, because I go to My Father.**
>
> *John 14:11-12*

> **And these signs will follow those who believe: . . . they will lay their hands on the sick, and they will recover.**
>
> *Mark 16:17-18*

Certainly, the working of miracles was a great encourager and a boost to the confidence of those who witnessed as shown by this prayer of the Church in Jerusalem:

> **. . . grant to Your servants that with all boldness they may speak Your word, by stretching out Your hand to heal, and that signs and wonders may be done through the name of Your holy Servant Jesus.**
>
> *Acts 4:29-30*

Are miracles a fool proof method of Recognition?

No. We are clearly told that miracles can happen but that what is taught by the agent of those miracles is not always to be trusted.

> **If there arises among you a prophet or a dreamer of dreams, and he gives you a sign or a wonder, and the sign or the wonder comes to pass, of which he spoke to you, saying, "Let us go after other gods which you have not known, and let us serve them," you shall not listen to the words of that prophet or that dreamer of dreams, for the LORD your God is testing you to know whether you love the LORD your God with all your heart and with all your soul.**
>
> *Deuteronomy 13:1-3*

Also we are told that Jesus Himself could not do many miracles on certain occasions and as such they could not be used as a means of testifying to His validity on those occasions. Jesus is "**. . . the truth . . .**" (John 14:6) and as such what He says is always valid. But the miracles or lack of them did not always represent His validity.

> **. . . He did not do many mighty works there because of their unbelief.**
>
> *Matthew 13:58*

Indeed miracles are shown by the Lord as not a full pointer to the validity of the person when He says the following about Judgment Day:

> **Not everyone who says to Me, "Lord, Lord," shall enter the kingdom of heaven, but he who does the will of My Father in heaven. Many will say to Me in that day, "Lord, Lord, have we not prophesied in Your name, cast out demons in Your name, and done many wonders in Your name?" And then I will declare to them, "I never knew you; depart from Me, you who practise lawlessness!"**
>
> ***Matthew 7:21-23***

Jesus did not deny the miracles; He denied the person who practised lawlessness. This He spoke immediately after talking about wolves in sheep's clothing (Verses 15-20). But, before I delve there let's stick with the miracles a bit longer.

The lack of miracles as shown is not a clear sign of a wolf in sheep's clothing per se. Neither is the abundance of them a sign that what is taught is to be fully trusted. They will point to a full gospel being preached, but not to any inroads the enemy may have in the lives of the individuals concerned. Jesus commanded His disciples to make more followers and to teach these new believers to observe everything He had commanded them (Matthew 28:19-20). In the same gospel we read Jesus' command to:

> **Heal the sick, cleanse the lepers, raise the dead, cast out demons. Freely you have received, freely give.**
>
> ***Matthew 10:8***

So the Word shows us that while there are followers of Jesus there will be miracles. But these miracles are a sign of

God's faithfulness, not of the person's trustworthiness. God is a free giver and answers faith.

> ... though I have all faith, so that I could remove mountains, but have not love, I am nothing.
>
> *1 Corinthians 13:2*

A good example of this in many individual believers' lives is speaking in tongues.

> Though I speak with the tongues of men and of angels, but have not love, I have become as sounding brass or a clanging cymbal.
>
> *1 Corinthians 13:1*

You can speak in tongues and have hate or resentment towards a brother. You can tell a lie one moment and speak in tongues the next – Because it is a free gift – An ability God does not take back.

> For the gifts and the calling of God *are* irrevocable.
>
> *Romans 11:29*

Whether you go on to fulfil that calling or make wise use of these gifts will depend on your desire for righteousness, not on the gifts and the calling themselves. A good example of this in scripture is Balaam of whom we are warned as Christians not to be like (see also Jude 11).

> They have forsaken the right way and gone astray, following the way of Balaam ...
>
> *2 Peter 2:15*

Balaam was a man who could hear God and who prophesied accurately about Israel. But, his love for money meant that he taught the enemies of Israel what to do to cause God to resist the people of Israel by their idolatry and whoredom.

> ... Balaam ... taught ... to put a stumbling block before the children of Israel, to eat things sacrificed to idols, and to commit sexual immorality.
>
> *Revelation 2:14*

And yet he prophesied effectively, and spoke truth of God's nature. Undisputed scripture came from his lips:

> ... he took up his oracle and said "... God *is* not a man, that He should lie, nor a son of man that He should repent. Has He said, and will He not do *it*? Or has He spoken, and will He not make it good?'
>
> *Numbers 23:18-19*

> How lovely are your tents, O Jacob! Your dwellings, O Israel! Like valleys that stretch out, like gardens by the riverside, like aloes planted by the LORD...
>
> *Numbers 24:5-6*

All good stuff: From a man whose wickedness went on to be a byword for a wolf in sheep's clothing in the early church. He could prophesy, but his love was not in the right place.

> ... though I have *the gift of* prophecy, and understand all mysteries and all knowledge ... but have not love, I am nothing.
>
> *1 Corinthians 13:2*

There is a balance to be gained here in that miracles are indicative of God's activity and can point to the agent as true. Nicodemus said to Jesus:

> Rabbi, we know that You are a teacher come from God; for no one can do these signs that You do unless God is with him.
>
> *John 3:2*

They were a cause for people to believe Philip's words and turn to Jesus,

> . . . they believed Philip as he preached the things concerning the kingdom of God and the name of Jesus Christ . . . and was amazed, seeing the miracles and signs which were done.
>
> *Acts 8:12-13*

But, since they are not given us as clear signs in scripture to identify wolves they need to be understood primarily as gifts of God and acts of faith without necessary reference to what is taught at all times. They are indicative that faith is present and active, but not that the person or, the teaching from that person, is necessarily wholesome in themselves. They are no foolproof testimony to the person or teachings who is the agent involved with the miracles.

What does the Bible say is a sign of a wolf?

Jesus said:

> Beware of false prophets, who come to you in sheep's clothing, but inwardly they are ravenous wolves. You will know them by their fruits . . .
>
> *Matthew 7:15-16*

This could be understood to mean that these are people who come from outside, but Paul makes clear that the very elders of New Testament churches are included. In his farewell speech to the elders of the church at Ephesus he said:

> . . . I know this, that after my departure savage wolves will come in among you, not sparing the flock. Also from among yourselves men will rise up, speaking perverse things, to draw away the disciples after themselves.
>
> *Acts 20:29-30*

From amongst them there would be those who would end up being as wolves in sheep's clothing. Those in leadership are not excluded. Anyone is in a position to allow the enemy to affect their life and through this become a wolf within the church. The only method of recognising these Jesus said is by their fruits. As explained above it is not the miracles which will help identify them. It is the fruits. It is not the sound or lack of sound teaching per se. It is the fruits: Although one such fruit as I will explain is often linked with doctrine.

What fruits?

Possible Answer: Charitable giving testifies to the validity of the Man of God?

Was Jesus talking about good deeds? Like giving to the poor? No. Since this is something that can be done without the right heart. It can all be done for show like the hypocrites Jesus mentioned:

> . . . do not do your charitable deeds before men, to be seen by them . . . when you do a charitable deed, do not sound a

> trumpet, before you as the hypocrites do in the synagogues
> and in the streets, that they may have glory from men . . .
>
> *Matthew 6:1-2*

These can be seen as a fruit when you realise the attitude in which they are done. The deed itself is no proof. But, the desire to give to and help others is a good fruit when honestly in a self-effacing manner and without show. God loves a cheerful giver (2 Corinthians 9:7). But, the regular open declaration that one does give to the poor is a fruit of an evil heart. It seeks the praise and recognition of men.

> . . . the pride of life – is not of the Father but is of the world.
>
> *1 John 2:16*

This can therefore be seen as a fruit to look out for. For without genuine love, charitable or allegedly generous giving is a sham.

> . . . though I bestow all my goods to feed *the poor* . . . but have not love, it profits me nothing.
>
> *1 Corinthians 13:3*

A good example of this "show" in giving is Judas Iscariot of whom John wrote about after Mary had poured expensive perfume on Jesus' feet. Just as it was a problem with Balaam, so it was with Judas Iscariot:

> . . . Judas Iscariot . . . said, "Why was this fragrant oil not sold for three hundred denarii and given to the poor?" This he said, not that he cared for the poor, but because he was a thief, and had the money box; and he used to take what was put in it.
>
> *John 12:4-6*

The handling of money is helpful to identify a fruit of a wolf. The attitude held and reaction to the gift of others, a good indicator of the heart. In fact the reaction to good news unconnected with your actions is a good indicator of pride – see the chapter on pride – A faculty always existent in an evil heart.

> **I will bless the LORD at all times; His praise *shall* continuously *be* in my mouth. My soul shall make its boast in the LORD; the humble shall hear *of it* and be glad.**
>
> *Psalm 34:1-2*

The proud shall hear of it and not be glad. This is talking of gladness of heart. It involves genuine love of the recipient's heart exercising joy. The proud instead will want to add to the story or, qualify it in some way. I have often found this particular fruit useful to identify and recognise where I am at in relation to pride. A prayer and a genuine desire to listen and take heed to the other person the way through. I explained this in the preceding chapter; it is here for the sake of those who have "jumped" to this one. If, on the other hand the fruit is prevalent then the door is open for the enemy to the heart of the individual concerned.

This tells us that outward show is also not a good indicator of a false person or teaching. Miracles are on their own, not a valid fruit "teller" and neither is a "good image", in terms of being an abundant giver.

The fruits

The fruits that show the wolf in the sheep are those against God's nature.

> . . . the wisdom that is from above is first pure, then
> peaceable, gentle, willing to yield, full of mercy and good
> fruits, without partiality and without hypocrisy.
>
> *James 3:17*

This wisdom displayed in the individual's attitude to life
and interaction with others shows them to be a Son of God.
But, what are the visible signs, the fruits of those who have not
this heart?

Isolation

If an individual in your flock, in your care is isolated from others
in the same group because they are treated differently then, this
is a clear fruit of a wolf in sheep's clothing. The wisdom from
above quoted above involves being "**without partiality and
without hypocrisy**". The act of isolating individuals is an act of
division of the church and is a work of the flesh:

> . . . the works of the flesh are evident . . . dissensions,
> heresies . . .
>
> *Galatians 5:19-20*

Disagreements are not the same things as dissension. You
can disagree and be in accord with the person: you disagree on
what they may say or think or feel, but you honour and respect
the person. But, any acts of rebellion to cause discord by either
party is a dissension. The leader who isolates for this reason is
equally at fault as the individual who sows his disagreements
amongst others. Love has regard for the other in being a family
irrespective of the differences. The moment either party causes
isolation of the other then this fruit is evil if nothing more

than temporary. It is proper to allow for a time of searching or evaluation, but this needs communicating clearly. Any extensive isolation beyond a reasonable period reveals the lack of desire for true fellowship on behalf of the one isolating. A period of say, more than 6 months to realise whether an individual is to be treated other than you yourself would be treated is not just unhealthy, but wrong. If a spreading of accusation has not occurred then the individual is for you not against you and to be treated as a full member of the family.

Accusation

This can take the form of accusation of individuals who are being isolated or other groups unlike your own. This is another classic fruit.

This accusation takes various forms. Mockery is one. Amongst your inner group the mocking of the individual isolated or, the group other than yours in sharing with your group are forms of accusation. One denomination or known grouping of Christians mocking or making fun of another group are effectively exhibiting a work of the Evil one.

> . . . that serpent of old, called the Devil and Satan . . . the accuser of our brethren, who accused them before our God day and night . . .
>
> *Revelation 12:9-10*

This mocking is a form of slander where self-control (i.e. of the tongue) is not present.

> . . . unloving, unforgiving, slanderers, without self-control . . .
>
> *2 Timothy 3:3*

This fruit is very apparent when the individual above who has been isolated or, when the other group is seen to have made a mistake or stumbled in some way. Due to the feelings within a joke or making fun at the expense of the other occurs.

> **. . . For out of the abundance of the heart his mouth speaks.**
>
> *Luke 6:45*

If we sought peace with all men then no such mockery would come from our lips.

> **Pursue peace with all *men*, and holiness, without which no one will see the Lord.**
>
> *Hebrews 12:14*

Exclusivity

This is the fruit of superiority. Pride in believing something you have makes you fitter than someone else. This may be because of a teaching you identify with or a practise. This is what idols and heresy do. Not only are these works of the flesh, but they are directly inspired and encouraged by the activity of the enemy. Anyone not submitting to this teaching or practise is isolated. Anyone championing the teaching or practise are praised and given credence. It is not that they are a fellow believer or family member that they are treated this way. It is in direct regard to the attitude towards the activity or belief in question. The moment someone says or declares a doubt regarding the "idol" then this person begins to be isolated and this fruit comes to the fore. With groups this causes a ghetto mentality to subtly develop. A clique amongst the inner faithful becomes evident. You often end up with a "high priest" of this which is being followed. Whereas,

> **Love suffers long *and* is kind; love does not envy; love does not parade itself, is not puffed up; does not behave rudely, does not seek its own, is not provoked, thinks no evil; does not rejoice in iniquity, but rejoices in the truth; bears all things, believes all things . . .**
>
> *1 Corinthians 13:4-7*

Although love rejoices in the truth it also believes all things. This is no reference to believing error or deceit, but to the way others are treated who themselves do no believe as you do. That is the test. How do you treat those who are in the Lord's family, but do not believe or practise as you do? Are you thereby exclusive in your practises?

Control

Control or domination are the fruit of a wolf in sheep's clothing. Jesus leads His sheep, He does not drive them. He does not order people about, He invites them to follow. He guides and instructs. And always leaves you with a choice because He has self-control. He works with you as a partner and a friend. The leader who leaves no room for partnership, but requires obedience without mutual understanding practises control. If in isolating someone others connected with this person are told accusations or directions to not associate with the individual then, control is occurring. It must not be forgotten that Jesus was known as a friend of sinners and publicans.

> **The Son of Man . . . a friend of tax collectors and sinners . . .**
>
> *Matthew 11:19*

Such that even if a church were to properly put someone out of their fellowship they are to play their part in remaining friends.

> . . . if he refuses to hear them, tell *it* to the church. But if
> he refuses even to hear the church, let him be to you like a
> heathen and a tax collector.
>
> *Matthew 18:17*

Not forgetting that if in the past some genuine sin had been done, when the person has truly repented then they are to be reaffirmed.

> This punishment which *was inflicted* by the majority *is*
> sufficient for such a man, so that, on the contrary, you *ought*
> rather to forgive and comfort *him*, lest perhaps such a one
> be swallowed up with too much sorrow. Therefore I urge you
> to reaffirm *your* love to him.
>
> *2 Corinthians 2:6-8 (cf. 1 Cor. 5:1-5)*

Control and exclusivity, let alone isolation prevent such a merciful act. Due to the room the enemy has in the sheep's clothing through which he manifests his fruits.

Who are wolves in sheep's clothing?

Well you and me actually. Whenever we open the door to the enemy we are in practise enabling the production of the fruits mentioned. Regular practise of these things causes us to become thoroughly deceived and unable to tell the truth in these areas of our lives. Wolves in sheep's clothing are not wolves who know they are wolves. They are sheep who do not realise the wolf they have become. Like the recognition of pride's existence mentioned earlier. These fruits recognised in any way needs bringing before the Lord to clarify His mind upon. Does He not say,

> "Come now, and let us reason together," Says the LORD, "Though your sins are like scarlet, they shall be as white as snow . . ."
>
> *Isaiah 1:18*

And John tells us,

> If we confess our sins, He is faithful and just to forgive us *our* sins and to cleanse us from all unrighteousness.
>
> *1 John 1:9*

But, before we can really see, we need to have our eyes able to see. Talking with the Lord about all of this is a top priority.

> I counsel you to . . . anoint your eyes with eye salve, that you may see. As many as I love, I rebuke and chasten, Therefore be zealous and repent.
>
> *Revelation 3:18-19*

WOMEN AND DECEPTION

In my book *Leadership is male?* one of the shortest chapters describes the difference between men and women. This is an essential part of understanding deception and why Paul advocated restrictions on the female gender in certain public sections of the assembly of believers. Once this is appreciated and catered for appropriately, there are no more hindrances to a full role for women in church leadership. It is my considered belief that any book on the issue of women in leadership without a thorough understanding of deception misses totally on what Paul wrote on the matter. Indeed, I have found the amount of space discussing deception in a book about the issue of women in the church is a tell-tale as to whether it is worth considering.

What I wish to do in this chapter is provide a stand alone explanation of the difference between men and women in regards to deception.

That there is a difference at all is explicit.

Paul wrote:

> . . . Adam was not deceived, but the woman being deceived, fell into transgression.
>
> *1 Timothy 2:14*

This is part of Paul's clear reasoning for having advocated:

I do not permit a woman to teach or to have authority over a man, but to be in silence.

1 Timothy 2:12

Leadership is male? has a whole chapter, related passages and an appendix to demonstrate this is better translated as:

I do not allow for a woman to teach, nor to exercise authority of a husband, but to be in quietness.

1 Timothy 2:12 JM

This helps to appreciate the relation to the next verse which is the other part of Paul's reason for what he advocated.

[Note: Paul says this in the context of the public learning and debating event (of the day when the speaker interacted with the hearers).]

Adam was formed first, then Eve.

1 Timothy 2:13

The creation order relates to the order of headship within the one flesh/marriage relationship. Further, Eve is told by God in Genesis 3:16 that her husband is to rule over her in matters related to any new intense desire which she is instructed to bring to him for that very purpose. This involved protecting her from future desire related deception. In *Leadership is male?* I explain the Genesis 3:16 command as the passage Paul was referring to when he said "**Let your women . . . be submissive, as the law also says.**" (I Corinthians 14:34) which in the literal Hebrew reads "**unto your man your desire and he to rule over you**" but, in the Septuagint (LXX), which was the version of Scripture Paul regularly quoted, there the Genesis passage reads "**thy submission shall be to thy husband, and he shall rule over thee**". This is why Paul mentions the headship as in the marriage setting as is well translated as follows (another separate chapter and an appendix).

> . . . and head of a woman the husband . . .
>
> *1 Corinthians 11:3 JM and Amp.V,*
> *GNB1&2, RSV, LB*

This distinct headship practise is also confirmed by both Paul and Peter when instructing "**Wives, submit to your own husbands, as to the Lord**" (Ephesians 5:22; 1 Peter 3:5) from which it is worth noting "their own husbands" as clearly meaning not to submit to somebody else's husband. But, in the Lord, we are all to submit to one another in the fear of God (Ephesians 5:21).

The main deal

However the deal is that before sin was a factor, woman's capacity to be deceived in a certain way is a reality to address and was revealed by the deception of Eve. Just as the capacity for passivity in a man's make up prior to sin's existence is a factor too and was revealed by Adam's inaction to obey the command of God, let alone by the reason for the imposition of a curse on the ground and it's later removal (Genesis 8:21). I discuss this passivity in the next chapter: Needing to be active in order to eat meant little time for the passivity of man, as fertile soil for the weeds of wickedness to grow.

How did the deception operate in the garden?

We see that Eve is described interacting in relation to what she experiences:

> So when the woman saw that the tree *was* good for food, that it *was* pleasant to the eyes, and a tree desirable to make *one* wise, she took of its fruit and ate . . .
>
> **Genesis 3:6**

In the short chapter I mentioned above I describe the difference between men and women as:

WOMEN ARE EXPERIENCE ORIENTED
MEN ARE TASK ORIENTED

We can see the enemy – Satan, the serpent (Revelation 12:9) – had fully observed how woman lived for experiences by her observations in speech and her actions. He took advantage of that by overwhelming Eve in what she saw, what she was about to taste and the benefits she would feel she would obtain from eating of the fruit. She was absorbed by her senses. We can see this overflowing feeling in the word for "**desire**" which God then described as the kind to submit to her husband for him to rule about in future in Genesis 3:16. The Hebrew word used is TESHUQAH with the core SHUQ being all about overflow as in "**the vats shall overflow with new wine and oil**" (Joel 2:24), "**the winepress is full, the vats overflow**" (Joel 3:13). This intense desire is not limited to human passion between lovers as in "**I *am* my beloved's, and his desire *is* toward me**" (Song of Solomon 7:10), but is equally the kind that sin and the demonic have to control and to rule us "**. . . sin lies at the door. And its desire *is* for you . . .**" (Genesis 4:7). So, is it any wonder they can impose and relay that desire upon us in order to make us fall in sin?

The thing is when a desire is intense, the emotional situation is such one cannot always think straight or, one can even feel unable to speak or, only to do so about and for the emotionally recognised in the moment. This is not a safe place if the desire is for something harmful or, if when felt in among others, it throws off the purpose of the group at a tangent. The time of the gathering is wasted.

But, in God saying to Eve (literal Hebrew) "**unto your man your desire and he to rule over you**" he is telling her that in the midst of having this desire, she still has the ability to submit it to her husband to make a ruling about. Thus providing a means to protect her in the middle of that desire: from acting on it to eat a newly offered fruit. In the absence of the man in her life, what is a girl to do? Simple, and this is true for the guys, for when the enemy equally imposes feelings on them, the answer is to wait. Do nothing new or different for a time. This is because anything from the enemy has a time limit on it for the simple reason that he does not have self-control and is not patient. Those are facets of the fruit of the Holy Spirit which they do not have in their rebellious make up (Galatians 5:22-23). But even in women waiting to ask their own husbands (1 Corinthians 14:35) – those who have them – they too may find themselves not needing to, as the intensity passes.

The other way is to discern by the very intensity and the compulsion in the feeling, that this is the enemy at work and not the Lord. Jesus leads his sheep. He does not drive them. God is gentle and willing to yield (James 3:17) and as mentioned he has self-control. The enemy does not. A tool in the armoury of the saint is to know and recognise the enemy's voice in this way.

As more of a task based person man lives in his head a little more and is more often deceived in the area of ideas and concepts. But in the middle of an active group of saints interacting with a speaker, to have the enemy prevent throwing off the purposes of the group or what is being taught by the Lord, in the recognition the female make up permitted experience related deception, Paul advocated for that time (in that time, for) women not to get involved. Which I believe is all he meant. Women were commended for teaching men (2 Timothy 1:5) and women (Titus 2:3-4). Interacting live in public in response to a speaker is another matter.

MAN'S 1ST SIN IDENTIFIED PASSIVITY AS HIS WEAKNESS

Following the creation of woman after man, a weakness in the make up of each gender then became apparent following the event of the first sin.

Paul refers to – as discussed in the preceding chapter – the existence of the woman's by saying:

> **And Adam was not deceived, but the woman being deceived, fell into transgression.**
>
> *1 Timothy 2:14*

At that point in time only Adam and Eve were around of the human race. Adam was not deceived. This is not to say he could not be, as men have been since, but that when they are, deception tends to work differently in men than with women. There is a difference.

What I am calling a weakness here is not as something that is wrong in itself, but an area of life that can be used as an access point by the enemy. Just as man's physical attributes mean that only a layer of skin protects from a thorn, hence the need for gloves, so also these weaknesses are only an issue when outside forces can be a danger.

The difference in woman is what enabled the enemy – Satan, the Serpent (Revelation 12:9) – to deceive her to eat the forbidden fruit. And, because it was out of deception she did this, she was blind to the truth that what she was doing was wrong.

The truth was hidden from Eve by means of her capacity to be overwhelmed, in an area of handling things connected to her perception of experience. The tendency to be more experience based than task based – more task based is what men are – meant that the allure of experiencing things pleasant to the eyes, good to eat and about to provide new things to her mind (Genesis 3:6) was too much to resist. This strength of desire for these experiences: I repeat women are more experience based than task based and, all these together: being pleasant to the eyes, seen as good to eat and, new knowledge to be gained, all thus overwhelmed her momentarily: So that, her logic and reasoning faculties by-passed, she forgot the truth. The truth was hidden from her for a moment by this deception mechanism. Young's Literal translation from the Hebrew reads:

> **And Jehovah God saith to the woman, "What *is* this thou hast done?" and the woman saith, "The serpent hath caused me to forget – and I do eat."**
>
> *Genesis 3:13 YLT*

This "**caused me to forget**" tends to be more often rendered as "to be deceived" as in "**The serpent deceived me, and I ate**" (NKJV). What Young's literal version (YLT) does is help us picture more specifically how this deception worked. It happened by causing Eve to forget the truth about the fruit being forbidden. This meant that in her moment of eating of the fruit, she was oblivious to her act being wrongful. This is where Eve now had an ongoing challenge to face. How not to do wrong things, which she cannot see are wrong things, "in the moment"?

And this I have discussed in the preceding chapter.

What I wish to highlight here is man's weakness, not woman's since that is already covered.

Adam's weakness

Since Adam was not deceived, then his eating of the fruit was a wilful act of transgression, unlike Eve's act. Hers was an act of transgression too, but not a conscious one (cf. Moses law in regards to transgression later realised: deeds done, but unconscious they were wrong when carried out – Numbers 15:28-29).

Since Adam was in a conscious knowledge this was wrong, what is it that can be seen to make Adam vulnerable to allow that act: to acquiesce to doing it?

I believe it was a form of passivity. A form of passivity that can thus be seen inherent in man's make up. It is man's weakness. We can learn and recognise this presence of passivity from what the Lord then put in place to counteract its effect.

Just as God brought in a new rule to counteract the danger inherent in what caused Eve to be deceived, to prevent further falls, so He also brought in a new rule in regards to man's own default weakness.

To the woman (not to the man about her) the Lord said, in literal Hebrew translation "**unto your man your desire and he to rule over you**" (Genesis 3:16 – See Chapter 18 from my book *Serious Mistranslations of the Bible*): in other words, submit to your man your desire so he decides in regards to its safety (right or wrong) "in the moment". As I said, these things I touched on this in the preceding chapter.

Since deception is the main issue and it is Paul's reason he wrote about the matters relating to women in church meetings, Paul's words, *without this appreciation of deception*, have been mistakenly used instead to cause leadership to be excluded as a role for women. This is as a result of missing out on the cause and reasoning Paul held. I uncover these in *Leadership is male?* I did not however then expand on the matter of passivity in man. This is my aim here.

God put in place new rules for life following the first sin

After the first sin, the Lord decided and put in place a number of new things. Of these, I wish to highlight two:

1.   A command to the woman to submit things to her husband: any new (overflowing) desire thus submitted to be decided upon, thus provided protection from new deception of this kind.

2.   A curse on the ground specifically mentioned as "**for man's sake**".

It is this last action that reveals the passivity in man.

This last action's relevance is confirmed in that 17 centuries after this curse on the ground was first pronounced, immediately following the Flood, the Lord then removes this very curse:

> **I will never again curse the ground for man's sake, although the imagination of man's heart *is* evil from his youth . . .**
>
> ***Genesis 8:21***

The removal of the curse on the ground here, including the repeated purpose "**for man's sake**" (Genesis 8:21), just as first mentioned when introduced (See Genesis 3:17 below), is linked to an explanation to which it relates: "**the imagination of man's heart *is* evil from his youth**".

This informs us that for man's sake, the curse on the ground somehow helped in the arena of evil.

How?

When the Lord first cursed the ground, he said what this would mean for man:

> Cursed *is* the ground for your sake; in toil you shall eat *of* it all the days of your life. Both thorns and thistles it shall bring forth for you, and you shall eat the herb of the field. In the sweat of your face you shall eat…
>
> *Genesis 3:17-19*

Because this is read in terms of hardship: as what is mainly pictured when read, rather than anything else, sight is lost of what this is really for. A punishment is felt as the deal here in such reading rather than something to be recognised as of benefit. But, since this very curse on the ground is then removed, connected with evil activity in man mentioned and, with the new permission now to eat meat also given after the Flood (Genesis 9:3), no punishment was intended. Instead, the curse on the ground was to assist in the area of man's idle thinking processes. To occupy your mind with the work involved to sustain life, was a help to prevent new evil decisions based on "why not?" out of this form of passivity (and he ate).

The curse on the ground at its introduction was a new requirement of the need to work persistently to survive. This has thereby been misunderstood as a punishment. Instead, by saying this was "**for man's sake**" – "**on thine account**" (G3:17YLT) – something else was intended. It was for man's good, not a punishment, that this was introduced.

Having to toil for sustenance – because of the curse on the ground – meant that no longer could food be easily found and thus, so much spare time as there was before, was severely diminished. A new focus and concentration with purpose (to survive) was now involved in the providing of nourishment for oneself and one's family. Notice also – I repeat – meat as food was not permitted until 17 centuries later.

All this activity thus provided a safer setting for man in the event of new occasions when a temptation to do evil arose. In the lack of activity and thus little forward going purpose evident, there is much ground for choosing to do evil. This is where the saying "idle hands are the devil's workshop" occurs. Paul wrote:

> . . . If anyone will not work, neither shall he eat. For we hear that there are some who walk among you in a disorderly manner, not working at all, but are busybodies. Now those who are such we command and exhort through our Lord Jesus Christ that they work in quietness and eat their own bread. But *as for* you, brethren, do not grow weary *in* doing good.
>
> 2 *Thessalonians 3:10-13*

It is not merely idleness that passivity encompasses, but not having a purpose and goal. That is what the curse on the ground addressed. It is not so much the physical inactivity that is at issue, but addressing a mental aloofness and lack of goal and daily purpose. Passivity tends towards detachment and apathy. A man lives more in his mind than in his experiences. He has both, but his prominent activity is in his thought life. So, with an open door to a wandering mind, room is found for evil imaginations out of pride: fertile ground for suggestions by the enemy (the Serpent and his minions).

This is why Paul advocates a taking possession of imaginations that are evil and casting them down and that, from our own minds (first):

> **For the weapons of our warfare *are* not carnal but mighty in God for pulling down strongholds, casting down arguments and every high thing that exalts itself against the knowledge of God, bringing every thought into captivity to the obedience of Christ…**
>
> *2 Corinthians 10:4-5*

Man's deception

The thought life is the ground where man gets deceived. An idea is placed there which, if allowed to remain unchecked for suitability (passivity), then becomes a seed or open door for attachments and a walk down a path of anything: from doing good that prevents the person to do what is best, or right on to just pure evil by a progressive belief that this is the only thing to do. See the earlier chapters.

It is because of this living in his head that a man can often be seen to be very happy on his own with his little project, hobby or idea. Whilst a woman with her life based more in experience is more often seen sharing these things…

The toil

We know the work required to feed oneself was significant. It can be seen by the stress put upon it when Noah's father – having learned and realised Noah was to usher in a new era (without this toil) – this is what he expressed:

> **Lamech lived one hundred and eighty-two years, and begot a son. And he called his name Noah, saying, "This *one* will comfort us concerning our work and the toil of our hands, because of the ground which the LORD has cursed."**
>
> ***Genesis 5:28-29***

Lamech prophetically named his son Noah. The word means rest/comfort/relief and this is connected to the new age Noah would lead mankind into: a new world with no longer the same toil required on the ground to produce sustenance.

> **Lamech named his son Noah, for he said, "May he bring us relief from our work and the painful labor of farming this ground that the LORD has cursed."**
>
> ***Genesis 5:29 NLT***

Lamech undoubtedly helped (it is highly likely) in the building of Noah's ark: When we add up the ages of the succeeding sons from the fathers and how long each patriarch lived (Genesis 5 and 6), we know that this saint was taken home 5 years preceding the Flood at the age of 777. The Flood date from Creation is 1656AC (After Creation); Lamech's death was 1651AC.

> **The righteous perishes, and no man takes *it* to heart; merciful men *are* taken away, while no one considers that the righteous is taken away from evil.**
>
> ***Isaiah 57:1***

I digress.

The prophetic utterance that rest from labour – respite from the toil – would occur, in Noah's life, happened: by both the Lord ceasing the curse on the ground and now permitting meat to be eaten for food (Genesis 9:3): all part of the new plan for life on earth following the Flood where no longer would vegetation alone be sufficient for food. New means to limit evil by man were also put in place. One rule for life removed, having been put in place for a purpose, now new rules were being put in: to take the place needed to cover the issue of limiting the growth of wickedness. Some new rules occurred during the Flood, some soon after and then, ongoing intervention was the norm to be observed through mankind's ongoing history. And, as further prophesied, this era will end with the King of kings on the throne: the final intervention.

The new limits (rules) put in during the Flood include the splitting up of the world into separate continents, new mountain ranges, new rivers and other such barriers to the influence and growth of wickedness by dividing an affected group of people from another. This was further aided by the giving of languages at the tower of Babel (Genesis 11 – another rule added following the Flood). Then, onwards, the Lord has used a nation by raising it to power, to limit new persistent evil from another nation – this has been done upon the people of Israel a number of times – and, other intervention types.

Okay, so, this removal of the curse on the ground meant man could now achieve great schemes whether good (magnificent edifices and other like with Solomon) or evil ones (the tower of Babel). But, no longer was man's passivity limited – disallowing evil imagination to bear fruit – by the toil, the necessary work on the ground for sustenance. The curse had been removed: All this points to man's passivity and his particular challenge in regards to deception.

IN CONCLUSION

The earlier chapter *Wolf in sheep's clothing?* I dedicated, when it was an article, to the late John Barr. He was an Elim Minister in Canning Town in East London. This whole book is now dedicated to John's memory. The deliverance ministry he headed was called *Freedom Road Ministries*: A great name. This name helps to view deliverance as a process involving the will of the person to be active in knowing and relating with Jesus as their God and Saviour. In the teaching part of this ministry John invited the authors of the classic work on practical deliverance *Pigs in the Parlor* , Frank and Ida Mae Hammond, to do some teaching. The Hammond book is so concentrated and full of information that it is not quickly digestible and with not a few things that require sinking in. Later on Frank wrote smaller books on Rejection and others, to help the reader with more palatable and faster beneficial consumption.

When I first wanted to put this work together on deception I envisaged a much fuller sharing with more examples of deception in the world and in Christendom. But, this would make this work unwieldy and less helpful than what this book is now: I trust and hope that it is a good door to this area of reality in life. There is enough to digest here already to furnish the saint with sufficient to make preparation and effective battle with the enemy.

I repeat the prayer from the end of the section on *The Characteristics of Deception*:

Dear Father,

Thank you that you are Light and in you is no darkness at all.

I ask that you shine your light in me and reveal all the beliefs and thoughts which I have taken on board as if from you, but in reality are not of you. I want to believe what is from you and nothing from the enemy. Just as you asked the church at Laodicea to anoint their eyes with eye salve that they may see, so I ask that you anoint my eyes that I may see. I thank you that the Holy Spirit will guide into all truth. I ask for discernment and courage to unlearn wrong things received as well as prevent new things which attempt to make a home in me. Help me to recognise any fresh work of the enemy which attempts to divert me from your ways.

Thank you that you give wisdom freely to those who ask.

Father I ask all this in Jesus' Name,

Amen

(1 John 1:5; Revelation 3:18; John 16:13;
James 1:5-8; John 16:23)